New Directions for
Higher Education

Martin Kramer and
Judith Block McLaughlin
CO-EDITORS-IN-CHIEF

Accreditation: Assuring and Enhancing Quality

Patricia M. O'Brien, SND

EDITOR

Number 145 • Spring 2009
Jossey-Bass
San Francisco

ACCREDITATION: ASSURING AND ENHANCING QUALITY
Patricia M. O'Brien, SND (ed.)
New Directions for Higher Education, no. 145
Martin Kramer, Judith Block McLaughlin, Co-Editors-in-Chief

Microfilm copies of issues and articles are available in 16mm and 35mm, as well as microfiche in 105mm, through University Microfilms Inc., 300 North Zeeb Road, Ann Arbor, Michigan 48106-1346.

NEW DIRECTIONS FOR HIGHER EDUCATION (ISSN 0271-0560, electronic ISSN 1536-0741) is part of The Jossey-Bass Higher and Adult Education Series and is published quarterly by Wiley Subscription Services, Inc., A Wiley Company, at Jossey-Bass, 989 Market Street, San Francisco, California 94103-1741. Periodicals Postage Paid at San Francisco, California, and at additional mailing offices. POSTMASTER: Send address changes to New Directions for Higher Education, Jossey-Bass, 989 Market Street, San Francisco, California 94103-1741.

New Directions for Higher Education is indexed in Current Index to Journals in Education (ERIC); Higher Education Abstracts.

SUBSCRIPTIONS cost $89 for individuals and $228 for institutions, agencies, and libraries. See ordering information page at end of journal.

EDITORIAL CORRESPONDENCE should be sent to the Co-Editors-in-Chief, Martin Kramer, 2807 Shasta Road, Berkeley, California 94708-2011 and Judith Block McLaughlin, Harvard GSE, Gutman 435, Cambridge, Massachusetts 02138.

Cover photograph © Digital Vision

www.josseybass.com

CONTENTS

EDITOR'S NOTES

We are all familiar with the Chinese curse, "May you live in interesting times!" It is no exaggeration to say that the past three to four years have indeed been interesting times for accreditation. Accreditation has long been regarded as an effective mechanism through which to assure and improve the quality of higher education, and it has long been accepted as a fact of life for colleges and universities. Although campus chief executive officers might occasionally bemoan the cost or the effort associated with accreditation reviews—and campuses that hold multiple accreditations are perhaps the most likely to voice such concerns—they were also quick to realize the benefits of the process.

With the convening of the Commission on the Future of Higher Education (known as the Spellings Commission) in 2005, however, accreditation came under attack. Two of the issue papers released at the request of the commission chair, Charles Miller, to support the work of the commission were highly critical of U.S. accreditation and, in particular, of regional accreditation. In "Assuring Quality in Higher Education: Key Issues and Questions for Changing Accreditation in the U.S." (2006), Vickie Schray from the U.S. Department of Education identified three areas of concern with regard to accreditation: (1) assuring performance: how accreditation can be held more accountable for assuring student performance; (2) open standards and processes: how the structures and processes of accreditation can be changed to be more open and more supportive of innovation and diversity in higher education; and (3) consistency and transparency: how accreditation standards and processes can be made more consistent to support greater transparency and greater opportunities for credit transfer. Although she offered no suggestions for changes to the accreditation process, the tenor of her remarks clearly indicated a belief that accreditation no longer served institutions or the general public well.

Robert C. Dickeson was even more pointed in his paper, "The Need for Accreditation Reform" (2006). He characterized U.S. accreditation as "a crazy-quilt of activities, processes, structures that is fragmented, arcane, more historical than logical and has outlived its usefulness" (p. 1).

In their critiques, Dickeson and Schray and others who support their point of view have taken many of the hallmarks of U.S. accreditation, characteristics generally perceived to contributing factors to its success, and recast them as scathing deficiencies. For example, U.S. accreditation is a process that is mission driven; it respects the tremendous diversity of institutional missions in this country. To be accredited, institutions must fulfill

NEW DIRECTIONS FOR HIGHER EDUCATION, no. 145, Spring 2009 © Wiley Periodicals, Inc.
Published online in Wiley InterScience (www.interscience.wiley.com) • DOI: 10.1002/he.330

accreditation standards, but they do so in the light of their mission. To those critical of the process, this emphasis on mission is interpreted to mean that the process is subjective and there are no hard-and-fast rules by which everyone has to abide.

Another hallmark of U.S. accreditation is that it is based on a qualitative as well as a quantitative approach to understanding quality. It welcomes qualitative measures of success as well as quantitative data. To accreditation critics, the lack of a well-defined set of quantitative indicators leads to judgments that the evaluative process is mushy and lacks rigor.

Furthermore, U.S. accreditation relies heavily on confidentiality, which is widely believed to be one of the reasons that it is so effective. Institutions can be candid in their self-studies, and teams can be honest in their assessments. Institutions can—and many do—choose to make public their self-study, team report, and the decision from the accrediting agency. But many believe that the fact that institutions are not required to do so is a strength of the system. Critics of accreditation characterize this reliance on confidentiality as secretiveness, an unwillingness to let those outside the academy know what is really going on. The fact that institutions are not required to disclose accreditation results—or that accrediting agencies are not required to disclose the results—is seen as a major impediment to the general public having access to needed information.

Another of the hallmarks of U.S. accreditation—that it is a process of peer review—is also viewed by many as a strength. Who better, one might ask, to evaluate the quality of a college or university than those who work in the field? In addition, the U.S. accreditation system is collegial: it is premised on the willingness of the institution to identify its own problems and propose solutions. The role of the team, then, is to validate what the institution has already identified as its strengths and areas for improvement, supplementing them with their own observations, of course. But the relationship is not adversarial. The evaluators are not inspectors coming in with their white gloves. Accreditation critics, however, see the peer review process as insiders taking care of each other—a perpetuation of the old-boy and old-girl network. The collegial nature of the enterprise is seen to give institutions too much power to shape how they are evaluated. Some would argue that a surprise inspection is a better way to determine institutional quality.

A final hallmark of U.S. accreditation is that a primary focus of the evaluation is improvement. The self-study and visit are not simply a compliance check as to whether the institution meet the standards. Rather, the focus is on improvement: Does this institution understand its own strengths and weaknesses, and can it develop and implement realistic plans to build on those strengths and overcome those weaknesses? To those critical of the process, this emphasis on improvement is seen as simply muddying the waters. Some would argue for a single-purpose evaluation process: Does the institution meet the standards?

In addition, recent critiques of accreditation have castigated accrediting commissions for emphasizing inputs over outcomes as measures of quality. Proposed solutions to the perceived shortcomings of the accreditation system have included severing the link between accreditation and eligibility for Title IV funding (eliminating the gatekeeping function) and dissolving the system of regional accreditation and replacing it with some kind of national structure.

While most in higher education who read these critiques would readily acknowledge the need for improvements to certain aspects of the accreditation process, most also agree that the critiques are, at least in some respects, outdated. Criticism that accreditation standards pay too much attention to inputs as a measure of quality, for example, may have been true fifteen or twenty-five years ago but has little validity today.

Guided by these issue papers, the report of the Spellings Commission contained recommendations that the accreditation process focus less on inputs and processes and more on outcomes, become more transparent, and make evaluation results available to the general public in such a way that interinstitutional comparisons would be possible. Furthermore, accrediting agencies were encouraged to set standards for student performance for the institutions they accredit. These recommendations were debated intensely during a period of negotiated rule making, which came to an end when Senator Lamar Alexander (R, Tennessee) called on the secretary to suspend the process while Congress finished its work on the Higher Education Act. (Readers interested in learning more about the recommendations from the Spellings Commission and the period of negotiated rule making that followed are referred to the archives of *Inside Higher Education* and the *Chronicle of Higher Education* as well as the Web site of the Council for Higher Education Accreditation.)

The Higher Education Act was reauthorized in 2008, and the most draconian of the accreditation proposals were not included in the final legislation. No national standards for student performance are anticipated, accreditation results are not expected to be used to compare institutions, the gatekeeping function remains intact, and no dissolution of the regional approach is planned. Critics and supporters of accreditation have weighed the current system against proposed alternatives, and all seem to have concluded, to paraphrase Winston Churchill, that accreditation in the United States today is the worst form of higher education quality assurance—except for all the others!

The chapter authors of this volume offer insight into U.S. accreditation—its history, values, advantages, benefits, and challenges—and in the process answer some of its critics. In Chapter One, Barbara Brittingham, president and director of the Commission on Institutions of Higher Education of the New England Association of Schools and Colleges, uses a thematic approach to understanding the development of U.S. accreditation. She outlines those aspects and characteristics of the process that make it uniquely American and describes the role of the federal government in shaping this non-governmental process of peer review. She reminds us that accreditation in the United States developed by "evolution, not design" and that its importance parallels that of higher education in general, both historically and today. Her comprehensive time line documents important milestones in higher education and accreditation.

Next, we hear from three campus chief executive officers: Patricia McGuire, president of Trinity University in Washington, D.C.; Robert Oden, president of Carleton College in Northfield, Minnesota; and John Bardo, chancellor of Western Carolina University in Cullowhee, North Carolina. McGuire, who has led dozens of accreditation teams, highlights in Chapter Two several of the advantages to individuals and institutions of serving on teams. Readers who have served on teams will likely concur with her characterization of such teams as "remarkable, albeit ephemeral" phenomena and will recognize the various roles of the team chair that she identifies: organizer, facilitator, coach, leader. McGuire tells a compelling story of how the exercise of these roles supported the remarkable turnaround at her institution. In stark contrast to the characterization of accreditation reviews as insiders protecting each other, she credits the challenging questions raised by the college's visiting team with providing the necessary motivation and needed guidance to support the turnaround process.

In Chapter Three, Robert Oden answers the question, "Does accreditation have any value for strong institutions?" with a resounding, "Yes!" He reminds us that at such institutions, accreditation functions as a valuable opportunity to view the institution in its entirety and is an effective catalyst to find the time to do what matters most. He underscores the importance of candor in the accreditation process and argues that the insistence on candor enables institutions to avoid "the temptations of becoming smug and self-satisfied or prideful or parochial."

Like McGuire, Oden has chaired many accreditation teams. Both acknowledge that such service is indeed a civic duty in higher education but also hold that it is among the best, if not the best, professional development they have experienced. In addition, both write about the satisfaction—Oden calls it the "inspiration"—that comes from working on a team and, as chair, from coordinating the "collegial, congenial" process through which a group of strangers becomes a functional team and accomplishes a difficult task in a short period of time.

John Bardo, who is a commissioner of the Southern Association of Colleges and Schools, reminds us in Chapter Four that the days when accreditation "dropped into" a campus once a decade are gone for good and that the current focus on accountability will not change with the new administration in the White House. He offers insights into the implications for campuses as they embrace what he calls this "continuous accreditation review" and consider what structures and policies need to be implemented and how best to deploy always limited resources. Bardo also tackles several of the thorny issues raised by the Spellings Commission—changing student populations, new instructional modalities, transfer of credit, and calls for heightened transparency and accountability—and discusses how accrediting agencies might effectively respond.

Frank Murray, president of the Teacher Education Accreditation Council, writes from the perspective of a specialized accreditor. He acknowledges in Chapter Five the "conflicting and incompatible expectations" that accreditors face and reminds us that those looking for accreditation to ensure the competence of graduates will be disappointed because the unit of analysis of accreditation is not the individual student but rather the program or institution itself. He goes on to describe how his association seeks to navigate these conflicting demands through a system that balances evidence of graduate competence with evidence of appropriate programmatic quality control and evidence of institutional capacity for quality. He concludes with several examples of the impact of his council's claims-based approach to quality assurance on the field of teacher education.

From Japan, Rie Mori offers an international perspective on accreditation in Chapter Six. She contrasts the U.S. system of accreditation with that of Japan and highlights both similarities—the importance of candor in the peer review process, for example—and differences, such as heightened governmental involvement in Japan. She traces the history of accreditation in Japan, with particular attention to the role of government in the development of that nation's quality assurance system. To those who would argue for greater governmental oversight of accreditation in the United States, recent experience in Japan offers several useful cautions.

In Chapter Seven, Judith Eaton, president of the Council for Higher Education Accreditation, presents a concise overview of the condition of accreditation in the United States today. In addition to giving a sense of the size and scope of the accreditation enterprise, she outlines the steps in the accreditation process that ensure that it remains a "trust-based, standards-based, evidence-based, judgment-based, peer-based process."

To close out the volume, Steve Crow, former president of the Higher Learning Commission of the North Central Association, draws on more than twenty-five years of experience to muse about the future of accreditation. He outlines a set of proposals for how the leaders of the regional accrediting commissions—the commissioners, board members, and professional staff—can regain the confidence of college leaders and public policymakers by reshaping the accreditation enterprise.

Crow's final admonition, "to lead," has relevance for all who care about the quality of higher education in the United States and who believe that this quality is best assured and enhanced through the peer review process of accreditation. During a time when self-regulation is often criticized, it is imperative that steps be taken to address the legitimate concerns raised about the ability of accreditation to function effectively and meet the needs not only of institutions but of prospective students and their families. The chapter authors remind us that if we in higher education do not take the initiative in this regard, it will be taken for us, and they propose several promising possibilities to pursue. Now it is up to us to implement these suggestions—in other words, to lead.

Patricia M. O'Brien, SND
Editor

References

Dickeson, R. C. *The Need for Accreditation Reform.* 2006. Retrieved October 8, 2008, from http://www.ed.gov/about/bdscomm/list/hiedfuture/reports/dickeson.pdf.
Schray, V. *Assuring Quality in Higher Education: Key Issues and Questions for Changing Accreditation in the United States.* 2006. Retrieved October 8, 2008, from http://www.ed.gov/about/bdscomm/list/hiedfuture/reports/schray.pdf.

PATRICIA M. O'BRIEN, SND, is the deputy director of the Commission on Institutions of Higher Education of the New England Association of Schools and Colleges.

NEW DIRECTIONS FOR HIGHER EDUCATION • DOI: 10.1002/he

1

*Accreditation has a rich history that has shaped its
purposes and processes.*

Accreditation in the United States: How Did We Get to Where We Are?

Barbara Brittingham

Each year on hundreds of campuses around the United States, thousands of faculty, administrators, and staff are preparing for an accreditation review. It is a process now accepted as part of the higher education landscape, and the basics are well known: a set of standards, a self-study, a review by peers, and a decision from a commission. But the development and context of accreditation are less well understood: How did we get to where we are? Where did this system come from? And how is it uniquely American?

This chapter discusses the conditions, trends, and events that help explain the current status of accreditation in the United States, focusing largely, but not exclusively, on regional accreditation (accreditation in the United States also includes national accreditors for faith-based and career-oriented schools and specialized and professional accreditors). What follows is not a history of accreditation (Bloland, 2001; Ewell, 2008), though an overview chronology of accreditation in context is provided in Table 1.1. Presented here are twelve points designed to show how accreditation developed in the United States—how we got to where we are.

American Accreditation in Context

1. **American accreditation is unique in the world.**
    With the international expansion of higher education, countries around the world are developing quality assurance systems to oversee both public and private degree-granting and other postsecondary institutions. The International Network for Quality Assurance Agencies in Higher Education began

NEW DIRECTIONS FOR HIGHER EDUCATION, no. 145, Spring 2009 © Wiley Periodicals, Inc.
Published online in Wiley InterScience (www.interscience.wiley.com) • DOI: 10.1002/he.331

Table 1.1. A Chronology of Higher Education and Accreditation in the United States

Date	American and Higher Education History	Accreditation
1636	Harvard College established by vote of the Great and General Court of Massachusetts Bay Colony	
1791	U.S. Bill of Rights reserves powers not mentioned in the Constitution "to the states respectively or to the people."	
1819	Dartmouth College case decided by the U.S. Supreme Court, preserving the right to operate chartered private colleges without state takeover	
1839	First state normal school started in Lexington, Massachusetts	
1847	American Medical Association founded	
1862	Morrill Act creates land grant colleges	
1870	U.S. Bureau of Education publishes an official list of colleges	
1876	Johns Hopkins University founded	
1885		New England Association of Schools and Colleges (NEASC) founded
1887		Middle States Association of Colleges and Schools founded
1895		North Central Association of Schools and Colleges and Southern Association of Colleges and Schools (SACS) founded
1900	College Entrance Examination Board founded	
1901	Joliet Junior College, first two-year institution, founded by president of University of Chicago	
1905	Carnegie Foundation for Higher Education publishes list of recognized colleges	
1906	Carnegie Unit developed	
1910	Flexner report on medical education, raising standards and leading to closure of nearly half of the medical colleges	
1913		North Central Association establishes criteria for collegiate eligibility
1917		Northwest Association of Colleges and Universities founded
1922	American Council on Education holds "standardizing" conference	
1924		Western Association of Schools and Colleges (WASC) founded
1925	American Library Association publishes list of accredited schools	
1926		National Home Study Council, predecessor to Distance Education and Training Council, formed
1934		North Central Association adopts mission-oriented approach to accreditation
1940	American Association of University Professors statement on academic freedom	

1944	GI bill provides direct funding to college students
1947	Truman Commission promotes network of community colleges, primarily for returning GIs
1949	National Commission on Accrediting (NCA) founded by higher education associations to reduce duplication and burden in accreditation
1950s	Accreditation develops mission-centered standards, self-study, team visit, commission decision, and periodic review
1951	NEASC gets permanent office and staff
1952	Veterans Readjustment Act ties financial aid to institutional accreditation
1953	Black colleges accepted as full members of SACS
1964	Federation of Regional Accrediting Commissions of Higher Education (FRACHE) established
1965	Higher Education Act (HEA) first passed, greatly expanding financial aid to students
1968	Formal process for federal recognition of accreditors established
1972	HEA reauthorization opens door to for-profit school participation in financial aid
1975	NCA and FRACHE merge to form Council on Postsecondary Accreditation (COPA)
1980	U.S. Department of Education started
1984	*Involvement in Learning* (National Institute of Education) calls for judging institutions by effectiveness in educating students; SACS adopts Institutional Effectiveness standard
1992	HEA reauthorization nearly breaks the link between financial aid and accreditors; creates National Advisory Committee for Institutional Quality and Integrity; authorizes state postsecondary review entities (SPREs) to review institutions with high default rates
1993	COPA dissolved by its board; Council on Recognition of Higher Education formed to take over recognition function
1994	SPREs defunded by Republican Congress; Council on Higher Education Accreditation founded
1998	No mention of SPREs in HEA reauthorization
2006	Secretary of Education Margaret Spellings's Commission on the Future of Higher Education publishes its report
2008	HEA reauthorized. Accountability for accreditation retained; secretary of education cannot regulate how accreditors judge student learning; advisory committee appointments to come from Secretary plus House and Senate

in 1991 with conference attendance from approximately ten countries; it now includes as full members 148 quality assurance agencies from seventy-five countries around the world. The list is a partial accounting of a rapidly growing phenomenon. But no other country has a system like ours; among quality assurance systems, the American system stands out in three dimensions:

1. Accreditation is a nongovernmental, self-regulatory, peer review system.
2. Nearly all of the work is done by volunteers.
3. Accreditation relies on the candor of institutions to assess themselves against a set of standards, viewed in the light of their mission, and identify their strengths and concerns, using the process itself for improvement.

2. The structures and decisions of U.S. government provided the conditions in which accreditation developed.

The U.S. Constitution, the Supreme Court, and the Congress each had a role in establishing an environment in which accreditation could develop. First, whereas accreditation in other countries is generally a function of the ministry of higher education, the U.S. Constitution provides that matters not mentioned in it are left to the states and to the people. So while the federal government has become more prominent in matters of education, the early development of the education system in this country was left free of government control, allowing the establishment of a diverse array of colleges and universities. The lack of government regulation also meant there was no clear and uniform floor on the minimum expectations for a college or a college education, leaving a vacuum that accreditation grew to fill. Thus, the social interest in having a sense of minimum standards was in part responsible for the development of accreditation.

A second defining act in setting the conditions for American higher education was the *Dartmouth College* case (*Dartmouth* v. *William H. Woodward*) in 1819, in which the U.S. Supreme Court effectively prevented the state of New Hampshire from taking over the independent institution and established the rights of private organizations. Daniel Webster, arguing before the Supreme Court, said that Dartmouth was a "small college and yet there are those who love it," illustrating the devotion to the developing institution that has been a bedrock of American higher education.

Third, that same era saw another important decision, this time by Congress as it declined to advance the legislation needed to begin a national university, despite the wishes of several of the founding fathers, including the first six American presidents (Snyder, 1993). Thus, the freedom of states, churches, and individuals to form institutions of higher education was ensured, and the basis for the considerable autonomy that American colleges and universities still enjoy was firmly established.

The U.S. Constitution also provides for the separation of church and state. By the time the federal government began significant aid to higher education after World War II, the country was replete with public and private institutions, both secular and nonsecular. The system that provides aid to the student and not directly to the institution accommodates both the Constitution and the desire to provide a broad range of student choice. By this time, accreditation was well enough developed that the federal government came to rely on it to identify those institutions worthy of federal financial aid for students.

3.   Accreditation reflects American cultural values.

Alexis de Tocqueville's 1835 *Democracy in America* is remembered in part for his observation that Americans form associations to deal with matters large and small. Accrediting organizations are one such example. The New England Association of Schools and Colleges was founded in 1885 by a group of secondary school headmasters acting in concert with a group of college presidents led by Charles Eliot of Harvard, gathering to consider their mutual interests in ensuring that preparatory and secondary school graduates were ready for college. Accrediting associations were established as membership organizations, supported by dues and fees (and occasional private grants), providing the foundation for self-regulation and the independence that has helped accreditation preserve the autonomy of institutions.

Americans value problem solving and entrepreneurship. As America expanded westward, settlers started businesses, churches, and colleges. By the 1860s, over five hundred colleges had been established, though fewer than half of them were still operating (Cohen, 1998). Tracing the early history of American higher education institutions is made more difficult because the term *college* might be applied to any number of types of institution, including technical institutes and seminaries. Indeed, one of the early tasks of the New England Association of Schools and Colleges was sorting out which institutions were in fact colleges, an undertaking made more difficult by the number of "academies" that sometimes spanned the boundaries between secondary and collegiate education.

Americans also believe in the ability of the individual to achieve a self-identified goal. Leaving aside the imperfections with which the belief is translated into reality, this optimism has proven foundational for the increasing access to education throughout this country's history, especially following World War II. The history of regional accreditation of various types of institutions of higher education reflects this increasing diversity of institutions of higher education and increasing access. For example, in New England, the roster reflects the first institutional accreditation in 1929[1] to twenty-one independent institutions, plus public universities in Maine and Vermont. Later dates reflect expanding access: the first state college in 1947, the first community college in 1964, the first for-profit institution in 1964, the first overseas institution in 1981, the Naval War College in 1989, and the first institution owned by a large for-profit education corporation in 2004. Examples from other regions differ in timing and type but illustrate a similarly

expanding base of institutions reflecting increased access to higher education. For example, the Western Governors University was developed in an
area of increasing population and large distances at a time when it was possible to envision an institutional model other than bricks-and-mortar to
expand access to higher education.

Accreditation relies fundamentally on volunteers to carry out the work.
Volunteering is, of course, a great American tradition: Americans volunteer
in schools, hospitals, fire departments, and settlement houses. Lawyers work
pro bono, and corporations volunteer executives to work with schools. In
accreditation, volunteers are at the core of the work: teams are composed of
volunteers, and it is volunteer peer reviewers who serve on the policy- and
decision-making bodies.

Americans also believe in self-improvement, an activity requiring self-
evaluation and identification of areas that could benefit from enhancement.
In accreditation, this value manifests itself in the expectation that the institution will demonstrate candor in reviewing itself against the standards. In
regional accreditation, the self-study process is not so much a proof exercise,
demonstrating that the standards are met (though they do need to be met at
some level) as an analytical exercise showing that the institution has the
capacity and inclination for honest self-assessment, the basis of self-regulation
and continuous improvement.

The Development of American Accreditation

**4.   Accreditation developed as higher education became increasingly
important.**

The history of American higher education is largely one of increased
access, mission differentiation, and experimentation. Accreditation is not
responsible for any of these features, but it has supported an environment
in which all three could flourish while providing a basic framework that pre-
vents chaos and promotes coherence in the system.

Harvard College was founded in 1636, and by the beginning of the
American Revolution, there were nine chartered colleges: Harvard University; College of William and Mary; Yale University; University of Pennsylvania; Princeton University; Columbia University; Brown University;
Rutgers, The State University of New Jersey; and Dartmouth College. The
lack of government regulation in the early years and the individual, even
entrepreneurial, nature of founding a college quickly led to more diversity
among institutions in the United States by the mid-1800s than many other
countries enjoy today. Table 1.2 summarizes the growth in American higher
education.

Yet the curriculum remained narrow, and the proportion of the age
cohort enrolled was small. In the late 1880s, 62 percent of college students
were enrolled in classical courses, and only about 1 percent of eighteen- to
twenty-four-year-olds were enrolled in college (Snyder, 1993).

Table 1.2. Growth in U.S. Population and Higher Education

Dimension/Year	1790	1870	1890	1930	1945	1975	1995	2005
U.S. population (millions)	3.9	29.8	62.6	123.1	139.9	215.4	262.8	295.5
Students enrolled (millions)	0.001	0.06	0.16	1.1	1.7	11.2	14.3	17.5
Number of institutions	11	563	998	1,409	1,768	2,747	3,706	4,216

Sources: Cohen (1998) and Snyder (1993).

In the 1890s, when the first accrediting associations were organizing, there were already more than nine hundred institutions of higher education, though the percentage of eighteen- to twenty-four-year-olds enrolled was about 2 percent. Institutions were small, averaging 160 students in 1890. But the economy was strong, the second industrial revolution was in full flower, America was in its (first) gilded age, and the link between economic development and higher education had been firmly established. The rapid rise in the number of institutions, and the types of institutions, increased the interest in a means of identifying institutions of trustworthy educational quality. Access was furthered by the establishment of land grant institutions, conservatories, black colleges, women's colleges, additional church-related schools, Bible colleges, art schools, military academies, research universities, and work colleges.

The rates of college attendance increased, though rather slowly at first. By 1945, 10 percent of the eighteen- to twenty-four-year-olds were enrolled in college; by 1953, the figure was 15 percent. By that time, the diversity of institutions had increased to include normal schools, business colleges, and community colleges. After World War II, the government made considerable financial aid available to returning veterans and required a way to ensure that taxpayer support was finding its way, through students, to legitimate institutions of higher education. Rather than develop its own system, government turned to accreditation, providing a major impetus for accreditation to develop its own enterprise.

By 1965, when the first Higher Education Act was passed, dramatically increasing the availability of federal financial aid, 30 percent of the age cohort was enrolled. The large number of baby boomers entering college at a time of social change provided the conditions for experimentation to flourish, for example, at Bennington College, Antioch University, New College of Florida, Oakes College at the University of California, Santa Cruz, the Experimental College at Tufts, and Hampshire College. The reach to accreditation to vouch for educational quality while providing peer oversight of responsible experimentation served both the public interest and the interest of higher education.

NEW DIRECTIONS FOR HIGHER EDUCATION • DOI: 10.1002/he

Thus, accrediting associations started at a time when there were enough institutions operating with essentially no government oversight that it was useful to begin keeping lists of what peers believed were legitimate institutions. (Developing later but somewhat in parallel are the national accreditors for career institutions, religious institutions, and distance education and a host of specialized and professional accreditors.) Accreditation became useful to the government when there was sufficient financial aid support to require a means of ensuring that the money followed students who were enrolled in educationally satisfactory institutions.

5.   Accreditation has developed through evolution, not design.
Following the beginnings of the New England Association of Schools and Colleges, other regions started similar groups: Middle States Association of Colleges and Schools (1887), North Central Association of Schools and Colleges (1895), Southern Association of Colleges and Schools (1895), the Northwest Association of Colleges and Universities (1917), and the Western Association of Schools and Colleges (1924). In the regions, accrediting associations tended to be started by the relatively well-established, highly regarded institutions, so as the membership increased, it widened from a base of highly esteemed institutions.

Although the New England Association was the first to be founded and had adopted standards of membership at least by 1929, it did not use the term *accreditation* until 1952, when it also initiated a program of periodic review. In fact, the other regionals, though using the term *accreditation* earlier than the New England Association did, also functioned for many years without a systematic program of periodic review now considered an essential element of accreditation.

The early years of accrediting associations are said to be focused on identifying which institutions were legitimately colleges. By 1913, the North Central Association had developed explicit criteria for membership (Ewell, 2008). The early requirements were uniform within a region and reflective of the time of cloth ribbons and manual typewriters—rather terse by today's standards, even as the landscape of higher education was becoming increasingly diverse. By this time, the country had highly regarded and respectable institutions of several varieties: independent liberal arts colleges; public universities, including the land grant institutions; and private research universities.

The tension between clear, stringent standards and increasing institutional diversity continued until 1934 when the North Central Association developed the mission-oriented approach to accreditation, which endures today. But producing a report, much less validating it by a team of peers, posed challenges: distances were great, roads in rural areas were uncertain, the era of roadmaps had just begun, and long-distance phone calls were expensive.

Between 1950 and 1965, the regional accrediting organizations developed and adopted what are considered today's fundamentals in the accreditation process: a mission-based approach, standards, a self-study prepared by the institution, a visit by a team of peers who produced a report, and a decision by a commission overseeing a process of periodic review. With the basics in place, the regionals have worked to refine and strengthen accreditation, learning from experience, and adapting to changing circumstances and expectations.

Since the mid-1960s, institutions have become more complex from an accreditation point of view. Driven partly by the requirements of federal recognition and partly from the realities of overseeing quality as institutions changed individually and collectively, accreditation has developed processes to train and evaluate team members and team chairs, oversee branch campuses and instructional locations, evaluate distance education, find accommodation for contractual relationships, deal with the related entities that accompany for-profit and some religiously based institutions, assume responsibilities for teach-out agreements when institutions close, and oversee the quality of campuses that enroll students abroad.

Also since the 1960s, the widespread use of information technology has enabled the development of a more sophisticated approach to data analysis, report preparation, and electronic communication. Photocopying and word processing provided new capacity for producing thoughtful reports. More recently, electronic spreadsheets, relational databases, e-mail, and the Web have provided a further foundation for the development of increased institutional capacity reflected in the accreditation process. The rise of institutional research as a field of practice has in many cases provided the human capacity to take positive advantage of the technology to analyze institutional effectiveness. Today accreditation can ask better questions and expect better analyses because institutions have the capacity to respond better than in the past.

More recently of interest is what may be considered a new generation of assessment instruments, including the now well-established National Survey of Student Engagement and its more recent cousin, the Community College Survey of Student Engagement, providing baccalaureate and associate degree–granting institutions with usefully comparable information on the educational experiences of their students. A more recent entry is the Collegiate Learning Assessment, which seeks to provide institutions with useful feedback on how much their students have gained in reasoning and communication skills and promising a measure of the value added by their institution in comparison with similar colleges and universities. More locally, electronic portfolios and consortia of institutions producing comparable data on student assessment enhance the ability of institutions to explore meaningful ways of considering what and how their students are learning, based on institutional mission.

6.   Standards have moved from quantitative to qualitative, from prescriptive to mission centered, and from minimal to aspirational.

The general trend in accreditation has been a movement from focusing on inputs or resources to processes to outcomes or effectiveness. Thus, there was a time when regionally accredited institutions were required to have a library of a certain size (at one point in New England, that size was eight thousand volumes, apparently regardless of the size of the student body or the nature of the programs). As accreditation developed, it became possible to focus more directly on ensuring student access and, later, student use of the resources and, later still, information literacy skills. Similarly, a focus on the credentials of the faculty was augmented by a concern for the quality of instruction. Leading and following higher education's shift in focus from teaching to learning, the emphasis of accreditation now is considerably on the assessment of student learning. This is not to say that the focus on inputs and processes should disappear. A well-qualified faculty is essential to quality in higher education. Rather, the focus on outcomes has developed to augment and shift emphasis in judging the quality of an institution.

When colleges and universities were being established at a fast clip, having minimal standards was useful in communicating, and ensuring, the basics needed for admission to the academy as a respectable institution of higher education. While there are still new institutions forming—in New England, the newest, Vermont College of Fine Arts, was chartered as this chapter was being written—the rate of establishing new institutions has surely declined as land has been settled and institutions of higher education have mastered the art of establishing branch campuses and new instructional locations and offering programs through distance learning. Increased requirements in most states for licensure and the need for accreditation's approval to have access to federal financial aid have raised the bar for establishing new institutions. Indeed it has become a challenge to ensure that the bar is not raised so high as to dampen the creative energy manifested in new institutions.

For established, stable, accredited institutions, minimum standards are of minimal interest. For accreditation to remain useful to these institutions, the process must have value. Accreditors have increasingly recognized that the process must promote improvement across the entire range of institutions. With standards at a sufficiently aspirational level, every institution finds dimensions on which it wishes to improve, promoting productive engagement in the accreditation process.

7.   Accreditation is a social invention evolving to reflect contemporary circumstances.

An application for membership in the New England Association of Schools and Colleges in 1932 reveals separate considerations for "senior colleges" and "junior colleges," and consideration of admissions requirements, graduation requirements, "recognition" from other colleges and universities, number of faculty (including the number with master's and doctoral qualifications and student-to-faculty ratio); hours of teaching per semester (minimum, average, maximum); departments in which instruction is offered; a statement of physical facilities "and a particular statement as to the library"; income from various sources and size of endowment; and total expenditures. The applicant institution is instructed that the "committee would also be glad to have information as to the makeup of the student body, and as to the purposes and plans of the institution for the future."

The separate handling of two- and four-year institutions is a matter addressed at some point by nearly all of the regional commissions: separate standards or different commissions were used to expand the operation to include two-year institutions in a manner that seemed reasonable at the time. Now, however, except for WASC, where two separate but cooperating commissions remain, the regionals have developed the means to accredit two- and four-year institutions, as well as free-standing graduate schools, with a single set of standards under a single system.

As accreditation developed, it embraced many of the essential elements of American higher education, including the role of the governing boards, the place of general education in the curriculum, the centrality of academic freedom for faculty and students, and opportunity for student development outside as well as inside the classroom. None of these items is required for federal recognition. (For the elements currently required, see subpart 602.16 at http://www.ed.gov/admins/finaid/accred/accreditation_pg14.html# RecognitionCriteria.) This disjuncture between what the federal government regulates, including "success with respect to student achievement," and the softer side of American higher education may help explain the angst that was generated by the work of the Spellings Commission.

That said, because a college education today is both more necessary and more expensive than ever before, accreditation faces new challenges to which it must respond. While assessment, understanding student success, and increasing transparency are the most significant issues, they are not the only ones. Accreditation has always changed as higher education has changed, and responding to increased calls for accountability is not the only current challenge for accreditors. Others include overseeing international branch campuses and instructional locations of U.S. institutions; determining what role, if any, accreditation has in student debt; and sorting through how accreditation deals with institutionally significant related entities, including large corporations owning accredited institutions.

Unique Aspects of American Accreditation

8.   As a quality assurance system, accreditation is unusually focused on the future.

From an international perspective, accreditation is not the only quality assurance system in higher education; others include academic audit and inspection, both of which focus more heavily on an examination of current or past activities to identify areas for improvement.

Accreditation as practiced in the United States focuses heavily on the future, on quality improvement, unlike systems built solely or predominantly to ensure the quality of the current operation and identify fixes that need to be made. Ideas for improvement can surely come from an examination of current practice, but they can also come from thoughtful consideration of societal trends, demographic projections, increased technological capacity, and a host of other sources. Accreditation is constructed to focus on the future, using all of these perspectives.

The various regional accreditors have different ways of emphasizing this forward nature in their self-study process. For example, SACS relies on a quality enhancement plan (QEP) to focus on improvement in an area of identified institutional importance; the New England Association includes a "projection" section for each standard in which the institution is asked to use the results of its self-assessment as a basis for planning and commitments in the area under consideration.

Awarding accreditation or continuing an institution in accreditation is a prospective statement by peers that the institution has demonstrated its ability to identify and address significant issues: that it is operating at a satisfactory (or better) level of quality and gives reasonable assurance that it will continue to do so for up to ten years, with specified monitoring, including a fifth-year report. Additional monitoring has become more frequent: for example, in 2007, the Middle States Association and NEASC specified follow-up reporting in between half and two-thirds of institutions undergoing comprehensive reviews, most often over matters of student learning, planning and evaluation, and institutional finance. Nevertheless, when compared with government systems in many other countries, it remains a light touch. The candor to identify areas needing improvement and the capacity to describe and pursue reasonable methods for improvement are keys to the confidence expressed in a decision to accredit or continue accreditation.

This forward focus of regional accreditation invites institutions to use the process itself for improvement. Standards that are aspirational allow every institution to harness the process to address identified concerns and enhance institutional strengths.

9. Accreditation has benefits not often recognized.

Some of accreditation's benefits are generally acknowledged: access for students to federal financial aid, legitimacy with the public, a ticket to listings in guides to college admissions, consideration for foundation grants and employer tuition credits, reflection and feedback from a group of peers, and keeping the government at arm's length through a self-regulatory process. Arguably these are the greatest benefits, but there are significant additional benefits as well.

First, accreditation is cost-effective. In 2005, regional commissions accredited three thousand institutions using thirty-five hundred volunteers in a system overseen by 129 full-time staff. Quality assurance systems in most other countries are more regulatory than in the United States and therefore more expensive. It is not unusual for a government-based quality assurance system to have, on average, one employee for every two or three institutions overseen. The Quality Assurance Authority in the United Kingdom, for example, has 130 employees to oversee the quality of 165 institutions. In the United States, accreditation has relied on volunteers from its beginning; NEASC did not have a permanent staff or offices until 1951.

Second, participation in accreditation is good professional development. Those who lead a self-study frequently come to know their institution more broadly and deeply; at a time of strong centrifugal forces in higher education, the self-study can draw faculty closer to their institution. Those who serve on or lead visiting teams often proclaim it is the best professional development they get. And the roster of presidents and provosts who serve the enterprise give testimony to its value. Outside of accreditation, few academics get the opportunity to see another institution, more or less like their own, at close enough range to gain a new perspective on their own work. To engage the theater of accreditation is to see the lessons of transformative leadership, capacity, mission, and governance played out on a stage of drama, with episodes of tragedy and comedy.

Third, self-regulation, when it works, is a far better system than government regulation. A regulatory approach can require institutions to report graduation and placement rates, but it is unlikely to engage the institution in formulating its own questions about what and how students are learning. Regulation seeks uniformity, whereas self-regulation is open to differences. Self-regulation does not always work, of course. Accreditation is challenged particularly in a time of low public trust to ensure that it retains the confidence of the public to oversee educational quality in a nongovernmental peer review system.

Fourth, regional accreditation gathers a highly diverse set of institutions under a single tent, providing conditions that support student mobility for purposes of transfer and seeking a higher degree. To be sure, there are some in the for-profit and national accreditation community who believe the doors of the tent are too often closed to their students wishing to bring credits or degrees to regionally accredited institutions. However, regional accreditation has gathered a vast array of institutions under a single system without drawing boundaries that inhibit transfer and leaving the decisions about the acceptance of credits and degrees properly in the hands of individual institutions.

10. Although regional accreditation may not be entirely logical, there are benefits.

Some of the regions make geographical sense: there is only one correct listing of the states that comprise New England. That said, given the North-South split of the country, the SACS territory generally makes sense, and therefore the Middle States Association as a region is understandable. The midwestern and western states that were not fully settled into statehood as accrediting agencies elsewhere were developed are somewhat less logically configured for purposes of regional accreditation. But then state boundaries lack an apparent rationale.

There are regional differences that impinge on higher education. In New England, we operate in a relatively small space densely populated with colleges and universities, so it is not surprising that there are no predominantly online institutions in our region. We will also face a demographic downturn among traditional-age students in the next several years that will place very different pressures on higher education from those experienced in parts of the country with expanding college-age demographics.

Accreditation is a self-regulatory system, relying on member institutions to form, adopt, and adhere to standards and policies. Regional commissions help keep the membership involved in accreditation by having more local opportunities for participation. Regions increase the ownership of the member institutions in the standards, provide communities of discussion that support knowing the standards well enough to internalize their meaning. And at some level, institutions must have internalized the standards sufficiently, through policy and practice, to be able to regulate their behavior consistent with the standards.

Regional accreditors vary somewhat in the terminology and processes, but overall, the enterprise is remarkably unified. Differences among the regionals reflect to some extent differences among the regions. New England has a strong tradition of independent higher education, and nearly half of its undergraduates attend independent institutions, in considerable contrast to other parts of the country. Many independent institutions in a region of small states raises the rheostat on issues of importance to nonpublic institutions. Conversely, the Northwest Commission operates in a region of large distances, highly dominated by public institutions.

Regional accreditation provides a natural laboratory for experimentation. As accreditation mastered the task of admitting institutions to membership while accommodating an increasing array of institutional types, it also began to wrestle with the task of making the accreditation exercise valuable for institutions for which meeting the basic requirements is not (likely) at issue and the related task of ensuring that accreditation fulfills its role of quality improvement for the full array of institutions. The regionals have approached this task somewhat differently. In the New England and Middle States regions, institutions are invited to propose self-studies with a special emphasis designed to align the energy of the accreditation process with key educational concerns or initiatives of the institution; visiting teams, while also ensuring that the institution fulfills the standards, pay special attention to the identified focus. WASC designed its two-stage process of capacity and effectiveness reviews largely in response to the needs of the large institutions that dominate the region (68 percent of students in the WASC region attend institutions of ten thousand or more students; in New England, that figure is 29 percent). SACS sequestered its compliance criteria to the first stage of its process and emphasizes the quality enhancement proposal element, and the Higher Learning Commission (North Central) developed the Academic Quality Improvement Program (AQIP) to provide an alternative process for institutions that prefer a continuous improvement model over periodic review.

The mobility of higher education presidents, provosts, and other academics encourages good ideas developed in one part of the country to find an audience for consideration in another part. Accrediting teams in many regions frequently include members from other parts of the country. Furthermore, strong presidential and academic associations, most notably the six major institutional organizations and (the late) American Association for Higher Education and now the American Association of Colleges and Universities, provide nationally structured platforms for academics to speak to their regionally structured accreditors. (These six are the American Council on Education, American Association of State Colleges and Universities, American Association of Community Colleges, Association of American Universities, National Association of Independent Colleges and Universities, and National Association of State Universities and Land-Grant Colleges.) Finally, the regional accreditors have strengthened their own cooperative muscles of late, united by proposals from Washington and, more positively, on joint efforts around distance learning and assessment.

Accreditation's External Relationships

11. Accreditation is in an evolving relationship with the federal government

With nearly $90 billion invested annually in federal financial aid, the government, representing taxpayers, deserves a robust system to ensure that the schools the recipient students attend are of sufficient educational quality. And in fact it was the increasing amount of federal financial aid that both increased access to higher education and led to the recognition of accreditors as the gatekeepers to federal funds.

The federal program to recognize accrediting organizations as "reliable authorities concerning the quality of education or training offered by the institutions of higher education . . . they accredit" began quietly. From what has been called the second GI bill, providing support for returning veterans from the Korean War, the federal government began to rely on accreditation organizations to identify institutions educationally worthy of taxpayer investment in the form of federal financial aid to students. Thus, when the Higher Education Act was first passed in 1965, greatly expanding federal financial aid to students, the government turned to accreditation to identify institutions eligible for student payment of this aid. The process was developed by 1968 and conducted initially by federal staff.

Viewed through the lens of federal financial aid, institutions were overseen by "the triad": states for purposes of licensure and basic consumer protection, the federal government for purposes of effective oversight of financial aid funds, and recognized accreditors to ensure sufficient educational quality.

At the beginning, the process appeared to pose no challenges to the authority of accreditation and therefore the autonomy of institutions. As late as 1986, the director of a regional accrediting commission described the relationship with the government as "benignly quiescent" (Cook, p. 166). But things had begun to change on two fronts: expectations for what has come to be called assessment of student learning and problems with the use of federal financial aid.

In 1984, a federal panel established by the National Institute of Education published *Involvement in Learning*. Arguing for access and degree completion, the panel also identified the need to focus more clearly on student learning outcomes. That same year, SACS developed a standard on institutional effectiveness, a move adopted soon after by the other regionals. These efforts built on an emerging body of research on student learning in higher education and helped spur the assessment movement (see, for example, Ewell, n.d.).

Meanwhile, the availability of large amounts of federal financial aid had attracted a few bad actors into the business of postsecondary and higher education. There were instances, most but not all outside the realm of regional accreditation, of institutions with high student loan default rates, where allegations of fraud and abuse seem not to have been misplaced.

The relationship between accreditors and the federal government changed abruptly during the 1992 reauthorization of the Higher Education Act. Most dramatic, Congress, distressed with high student loan default rates and frustrated that accreditors were not taking action, at one point considered breaking the link between accreditation and federal financial aid to students. Instead the reauthorized act included the establishment of state postsecondary review entities (SPREs), which would have had states conduct reviews based on stringent quantitative criteria in instances triggered by high institutional loan default rates. The SPREs also gave states the authority to conduct investigations where they had reason to believe there were problems. The threat was never realized: the 1994 Republican Congress declined to fund the SPREs, and they were written out of the law during the 1998 reauthorization.

The discussion of the SPREs highlighted the very differing capacities of states to oversee basic quality in higher education and their enthusiasm for undertaking the role with respect to independent higher education. Some states have robust processes to oversee the quality of independent as well as public higher education, some have satisfactory licensing processes to establish an effective floor, and some now outsource quality assurance by requiring accreditation by a regional accreditor or other federally recognized body. But a few states—fortunately a decreasing number—have declined to set a reasonable minimum bar for operation, attracting institutions of minimal quality or, in some cases, degree mills.

NEW DIRECTIONS FOR HIGHER EDUCATION • DOI: 10.1002/he

The 1992 reauthorization also upped the ante on student learning assessment. The bill specified areas that accreditors needed to include in their standards and reviews, including curriculum, faculty, and student achievement. The new bill established the National Advisory Committee for Institutional Quality and Integrity (NACIQI) as the group making recommendations to the secretary of education regarding the recognition of accrediting agencies; staff now provide the background information and make a recommendation to NACIQI. That members of NACIQI are appointed by the secretary of education raises concerns about the extent to which political agendas have been pursued, however.

As the government engaged accreditors on the matter of assessment, the engagement was generally in line with accreditation's approach to assessment, that is, as a means of providing evidence useful for institutional improvement. But the game seemed to change when the Commission on the Future of Higher Education, established by Secretary of Education Margaret Spellings (and referred to as the Spellings Commission), issued its report in 2006; the administration and its supporters were highly critical of accreditation for not providing "solid evidence, comparable across institutions, of how much students learn in colleges or whether they learn more at one college than another" (p. 13).

The atmosphere for increased federal concern, if not scrutiny of academic quality in higher education, is influenced by two recent trends:

- Higher education is more important than ever before. For individuals, the route to the middle class relies increasingly on higher education. Over a lifetime, a worker with a bachelor's degree has estimated earnings nearly twice that of a high school graduate.
- Higher education is more expensive than ever before in terms of both direct cost during the college years and the accumulation of debt upon leaving higher education. By 2006, approximately two-thirds of students with a bachelor's degree graduated with debt that averaged nearly twenty thousand dollars (Project on Student Debt, 2007).

As the Higher Education Act becomes more complex (the 2008 version runs over eleven hundred pages) and the experience of recognition surfaces new issues that the Department of Education seeks to address, the regulation surrounding the recognition of accreditors has intensified. This recognition system has become increasing complex—and some would say intrusive into the business of accreditation. How the regulation is carried out also matters; the approach taken by Secretary Spellings, bolstered by the report of her Commission on the Future of Higher Education, was activist, changing the atmosphere and raising the stakes (Lederman, 2007).

Peter Ewell (2008) has identified a major cause of the tension between federal regulators and accreditors as the "the principal-agent problem." In this case, the principal is the federal government, and the agent is the accreditor, authorized to carry out a quality assurance function on behalf of the principal. Because the agent, the accreditor, is close to the institutions whose quality it oversees, it is "captured" and imperfectly fulfills the expectations of the principal. But accreditors do not think of their primary role as federal agents. Thus, the agendas of the principal and the actors are not entirely congruent, resulting in a heightened desire for control—regulation—on the part of the government-as-agent and a reluctance on the part of accreditors to assume additional regulatory functions in their relationships with colleges and universities.

The 2008 version of the Higher Education Act does not permit the secretary of education to regulate the portions of the law on how accreditors should specify and examine institutions with respect to student achievement. And NACIQI will be restructured so that members are appointed equally by the secretary of education, the House, and the Senate, the latter two with bipartisan members. Given the importance and expense of a college education, however, the importance of understanding the educational effectiveness of institutions will not abate. And the Higher Education Act is reauthorized every five years, so there is every reason to believe this saga will continue.

12. Colleges and universities are the members of accrediting associations and also influence accreditation through their other membership organizations.

The national presidentially based professional associations have had a long history of working to coordinate, oversee, and reduce the "burden" of accreditation on member institutions. As accreditation developed, some of the larger, more complex institutions were being visited not only by their regional accreditor but also a growing number of specialized accreditors. In 1949 a group of higher education associations formed the National Commission on Accreditation, with the goal of reducing the duplication and burden to institutions resulting from multiple accreditors.

About the same time, the regional accreditors joined together to create the National Commission on Regional Accrediting Agencies, replaced in 1964 by the Federation of Regional Accrediting Commissions of Higher Education (FRACHE). In 1975, in an attempt to create a strong central authority for accreditation, FRACHE, which by then included some of the national accreditors of career schools, and the National Commission joined forces to create the Council on Postsecondary Accreditation (COPA).

One of COPA's most visible activities was the development of a process to recognize accreditors. The process had two main goals. The first was to ensure that accreditors comported themselves suitably in their relations with institutions. For example, provision was made to ensure that accreditors initiated an accreditation review only on the invitation of the institution's chief executive officer. Process requirements ensured that the institution had an opportunity to review a draft accreditation report and ensure it was factually correct. The second purpose was to guard against what the presidential associations saw as the proliferation of accrediting associations, as new groups were being established and seeking their legitimate place at the table. This goal proved challenging, as there was external and considerable institutionally based support for a continuing parade of new specialized accreditors.

Upon legal advice, COPA determined that it must entertain the application of any accreditor that met its requirements for recognition regardless of whether there was an existing accreditor in that field. Somewhat to the dismay of the presidents, this meant that not only was there less likelihood of holding new accreditors at arm's length, but also that there could be multiple accreditors in a field. Today there are multiple accreditors in business, nursing, and education. Interestingly, while presidents and provosts have at times resisted the establishment of new specialized accreditors, as assessment and the understanding of student learning outcomes has become more important, it is often the professional programs, pushed by these same accreditors, that have experience valuable to their campus colleagues on how and how not to approach assessment.

COPA's governing board voted to dissolve the organization in 1993. The various components served by COPA—the presidents and the several types of accreditors—were not working well together, and all parties were dissatisfied with how COPA had represented accreditation during the reauthorization of the Higher Education Act. COPA's task in the reauthorization was particularly difficult at the time because some of the national institutional accreditors that it recognized oversaw for-profit institutions with high default rates and the major source of the "fraud and abuse" concerns. Thus, COPA was challenged to have a clear voice representing all of its constituents.

The demise of COPA threatened to leave a vacuum. The Commission on Recognition of Postsecondary Accreditation (CORPA) was created to continue the recognition function, essentially picking up that process where COPA left off. Establishment of a broader organization was first attempted by the National Policy Board, a group of regional accreditors and major higher education associations, but the group could not reach consensus. In 1995, the Presidents Work Group was established to propose a national organization concerned with accreditation. In an institutional referendum, 54 percent of institutions voted, and among those, 94 percent voted to create the Council for Higher Education Accreditation (CHEA) (Glidden, 1996).

Unlike its predecessor, CHEA is an organization of institutions accredited by a recognized accreditor for which 50 percent or more of its institutions are degree granting. (This definition excludes some of the national institutional accreditors, giving CHEA greater focus than COPA had but making it more difficult for CHEA to be the overall convener of accrediting organizations.) CHEA has taken over the role of nongovernmental recognition of accrediting organizations, a role valued for providing access to a legitimizing recognition function for higher education accreditors that are not federally recognized. To be eligible for federal recognition, accreditors must be gatekeepers to federal funds, generally but not exclusively Title IV. Earlier, the recognition process was open to all accreditors, including accreditors of K-12 schools, and then all postsecondary accreditors. (ABET, the engineering accreditor, withdrew from federal recognition in 2001, believing its move to emphasize outcomes assessment was not compatible with federal requirements.) CHEA has also played an active role in the reauthorization of the Higher Education Act, has an active program of publication and organizes meetings that serve as the major national forum for academics, accreditors, government officials, the press, and international guests to discuss matters related to accreditation in the United States.

After the demise of COPA, the accreditors organized themselves into mission-alike groups. The regional accreditors regrouped into the Council for Regional Accrediting Commissions (C-RAC) providing a forum for cooperation, professional development, and external relations. C-RAC executives meet three or more times a year, once with commission chairs; and the professional staff hold a retreat every two to three years. C-RAC has developed policies and other statements on assessment, the mutual recognition of accreditation decisions, and the review of distance education. Periodically C-RAC meets with the Association of Professional and Specialized Accreditors to discuss topics of mutual interest.

The recognition criteria of CHEA and the U.S. Department of Education differ. Consider, for example, the contrast between the requirement by CHEA that accreditors notify the public of their decisions—that the accreditor has "policies and procedures to notify the public" of its decisions—with the regulation by the government, stated in 375 words, including the prompt notification of government authorities. Similarly, the requirements for accreditor oversight of branch campuses and instructional locations have increased dramatically, a topic about which CHEA recognition is silent.

With the secretary of education's role on regulating how accreditors approach student learning outcomes limited by the 2008 requirements, the door is open to CHEA, as a voluntary higher education body, to address the matter more in keeping with the traditions of self-regulation and good practice in accreditation.

Conclusion

Accreditation developed within the freedoms given higher education as the United States developed. Reflecting the American culture, accreditation has provided the context in which America's prized diversity of colleges and universities has developed. For half a century, accreditation, still changing, has provided a buffer between institutions of higher education and government, providing student access to federal financial aid while significantly preserving institution autonomy. Now, at a time of change in the economy, technology, and the federal government, accreditation has the opportunity to assess its status and context and prepare for its future.

Note

1. When NEASC began its accreditation program in 1952, the institutions previously accepted into membership were grandfathered and cycled into a new program of periodic review.

References

Bloland, H. *Creating the Council for Higher Education Accreditation (CHEA)*. Washington, D.C.: ACE/Oryx Press. 2001.

Cohen, A. M. *The Shaping of American Higher Education: Emergence and Growth of the Contemporary System*. San Francisco: Jossey-Bass, 1998.

Cook, C. M. "Commission on Institutions of Higher Education." In *The First Hundred Years: 1885–1985*. Bedford, Mass.: New England Association of Schools and Colleges, 1986.

Ewell, P. T. *U.S. Accreditation and the Future of Quality Assurance: A Tenth Anniversary Report from the Council for Higher Education Accreditation*. Washington, D.C.: Council for Higher Education Accreditation, 2008.

Ewell, P. T. *An Emerging Scholarship: A Brief History of Assessment*. n.d. Retrieved December 8, 2008 from http://www.scup.org/pdf/webcast/A_Brief_History_of_Assessment-Peter%E2%80%A6.pdf.

Glidden, R. "Accreditation at the Crossroads." *Educational Record,* Fall 1996, pp. 22–24. Retrieved October 1, 2008 from http://www.chea.org/Research/crossroads.cfm. October 8, 2008 from http://www.insidehighered.com/news/2007/12/14/accredit.

Lederman, D. "Lack of Consensus on Consensus." *Inside Higher Ed,* June 4, 2007. Retrieved October 8, 2008 from http://insidehighered.com/news/2007/06/04/accredit.

National Institute of Education, Study Group on the Conditions of Excellence in American Higher Education. *Involvement in Learning: Realizing the Potential of American Higher Education*. Washington, D.C.: U.S. Government Printing Office, 1984.

Project on Student Debt. "Student Debt and the Class of 2006." 2007 Retrieved October 8, 2008 from http://projectonstudentdebt.org/files/pub/ State_by_State_report_FINAL.pdf.

Synder, T. D. (ed.). *120 Years of American Education: A Statistical Portrait*. Washington, D.C.: National Center for Educational Statistics, 1993.

U.S. Department of Education. *A Test of Leadership: Charting the Future of U.S. Higher Education*. Washington, D.C.: U.S. Department of Education, 2006.

U.S. Department of Education, Database of Accredited Postsecondary Institutions and Programs. Retrieved December 6, 2008 from http://ope.ed.gov/accreditation/Glossary.aspx.

BARBARA BRITTINGHAM *is the president/director of the Commission on Institutions of Higher Education of the New England Association of Schools and Colleges.*

2

The accreditation process helped a small, private university move from crisis to success.

Accreditation's Benefits for Individuals and Institutions

Patricia A. McGuire

Participation in accreditation processes, on visiting teams as well as through institutional self-study, is an excellent opportunity for individual academics to augment their professional expertise in a range of higher education issues: strategic planning and assessment, resource management and capital investments, curriculum planning and program development, and academic and corporate governance. At the same time, robust engagement with accreditation processes can help colleges and universities address challenging issues through using planning and self-study to drive institutional change.

This chapter first considers the benefits of participation on accreditation teams for members and the chair. It then presents a case study on the role that accreditation played in moving one institution from crisis to success.

The Accreditation Team

Each year thousands of administrators and faculty members volunteer countless labor hours to conduct accreditation reviews for colleges and universities. The heart of this enterprise is the accreditation team itself: a small group of peers from other institutions who come together to assess a college's compliance with accreditation standards. Assembling an accreditation team is no small task; with a broad diversity of institutional types in higher education today, accreditation staff must carefully match volunteers with experience in similar settings: a small women's college, for example, needs a different kind of team than a large public university does, and specialized, technical, or proprietary institutions often need unique expertise as well.

NEW DIRECTIONS FOR HIGHER EDUCATION, no. 145, Spring 2009 © Wiley Periodicals, Inc.
Published online in Wiley InterScience (www.interscience.wiley.com) • DOI: 10.1002/he.332

Accreditation teams are remarkable, albeit ephemeral, social structures. A group of strangers comes together for a few days to conduct a probing review of an institution they have come to know only through the self-study. Between late Sunday afternoon, when the members typically first assemble, and Wednesday noon, when the group dissolves and flies off to their respective home campuses, the individuals must cohere into a functional team speaking with one voice, writing a singular report, and assessing institutional compliance with accreditation standards according to commonly accepted modes of institutional performance measurement.

Teamwork and singularity of voice are rare virtues in academia, so the potential for some dysfunction on the visiting team is considerable. Yet most of the time, the process works well, thanks to the professionalism of team members and the skill of the team chair. Team members spend long days interviewing campus constituents, reviewing documents, and analyzing the self-study and other evidence collected during the visit; then they spend even longer nights engaged in dispassionate and thoughtful group analysis of the evidence in the light of the accreditation standards. In the intense short life of a visiting team, the qualities of collegiality and congeniality are vital to the effectiveness of the team.

Why should a faculty member or administrator agree to serve on an accreditation team? The most obvious reason is academic civic duty: volunteering time for accreditation work is an obligation of citizenship in the land of higher education. A second obvious reason is self-protection: academics must "own" voluntary peer review robustly, or others (federal or state governments) will assume accreditation roles with less effective, more burdensome regulatory behavior.

But beyond the obvious notions of civic duty and institutional self-interest, participants can reap benefits that will be useful at their home campuses. While an absolute rule of team participation is that team members should not compare the institution under study to their own institutions, the reality is that a personal frame of reference is essential to understand the subject of the study. Without blurting out the obvious comparison ("Oh, that's *just like* our first-year program," or "On *my* campus, we require faculty office hours every day"), team members are continuously absorbing and analyzing information that for the most part is quite familiar in its essence, though the application may well be quite different. Service on a visiting team allows a faculty member or dean to observe an unfamiliar program in practice, learn about new assessment methods, and see new designs for libraries and laboratories. Administrators on teams can hear colleagues discuss best practices for student services or human resource management or take a look at innovations in residence life or facilities management. Beyond learning about innovative courses or new approaches to enrollment development, a good team experience also leaves the participants with a few new professional colleagues who have shared the somewhat arcane experience of the midnight debate over whether the institutional documents reveal a genuine assessment plan (thus satisfying accreditation standards) or only an intent to think about assessment at some unknown future date (thus leading to a warning that the institution might not be in compliance).

The Role of the Team Chair

After the first day on campus, the visiting team will probably want to "shut the place down." Enter the team chair. Creating the teamwork dynamic within a disparate group of academics in a concise period of time while under extreme public scrutiny on the campus being examined requires a team chair who can operate with diplomacy, patience, good humor, and a firm hand with colleagues. Accrediting agencies frequently invite presidents or provosts to chair visiting teams on the theory that these leaders possess the industry knowledge, leadership talent, and stamina necessary to build and manage accreditation teams effectively. Chairing a team can test those skills considerably. The team chair must fulfill three distinct roles.

Organizer. The team chair is responsible for organizing the visit in cooperation with the institution under review. This includes everything from conducting a preliminary visit to determine the institution's readiness for accreditation to checking out the hotel facilities and dining options.

Facilitator and Coach. The team chair has to coach everyone involved about how the process works and then make sure that the process actually does work that way throughout the visit. The chair has to keep the team within the boundaries of the accreditation rules and protocols while being sure to encourage thorough evaluation. "Compassionate rigor" is a key phrase to indicate the necessary balance. Every team seems to have at least one member who is looking for scandal in every presidential decision and another member who refuses to think any bad thoughts; the chair must coach each extreme toward the commonsense middle. The chair also has to keep the institutional president informed and, at times, calm, since accreditation visits create some levels of stress at even the best of universities. Invariably, if the institution under review is a genuine college or university, some member of the faculty or student body will demand a special and "secret" meeting with the team to "expose what's *really* happening" on the campus. The president gets agitated. An effective chair tells the agitated president to take a long walk, gives all constituents an opportunity to be heard, and makes sure that the individual team member exploring the fringe does not lend undue credence to isolated cases of unhappiness.

Leader. Chairing an accreditation team is a role with considerable authority and responsibility. The reputation and future direction of the institution may well hinge on the team report, and the chair represents to the campus community the face of a final judgment culminating years of hard work in self-study. The fact that the final judgment is really made by a commission

NEW DIRECTIONS FOR HIGHER EDUCATION • DOI: 10.1002/he

of other people who will assemble months hence is beside the point. To the institution under review, the team chair *is* the accrediting commission. While in most cases, the team chair's role is more benevolent than threatening, in some cases the team chair must assume the persona of Leviathan in order to move the institution to the right place. Sometimes a team chair has to tell a president that the institution's self-study is completely inadequate and must be redone; in another case, a team chair may need to warn the board of trustees that their inattention to a serious internal conflict between the president and faculty is harming the college. With a well-chosen blend of stern words and firm guidance at the right times, a good chair can move an institution away from self-inflicted damage and back onto a pathway toward reaccreditation. Several team chairs did just that in the case study in this chapter.

A Note About the Federal Role in Accreditation

Although the Higher Education Opportunity Act of 2008 (Reauthorization Act) did not substantially change the current federal oversight role in accreditation, the law does open the door for increased scrutiny of accreditation processes and possible public exposure of accreditation reports. Critics of accreditation, who claim that the process is too insular, did not convince Congress to replace the vast networks of voluntary peer review with direct federal intervention in the accreditation of institutions. However, the net result of the accreditation debates is a heightened awareness on the part of team members and chairs that their work occurs in a fishbowl. Knowing that regulators and the public are paying closer attention to the quality and dispassionate rigor of accreditation processes and reports, team chairs have an even greater responsibility to ensure that all phases of the accreditation review meet the highest standards for insightful analysis of institutional conditions, findings supported by clear evidence, and written reports that can stand up to public scrutiny.

Case Study: Accreditation's Role in Trinity's Renaissance

This case study examines how accreditation processes over a period of time helped one college to move from crisis to renaissance. The institution is Trinity in Washington, a historic Catholic women's college now operating as a diversified comprehensive university. (I have been president of Trinity since 1989 and a trustee since 1986. I am a 1974 graduate of Trinity. Trinity's accreditation reports are available on its Web site: www.trinitydc.edu.)

The Sisters of Notre Dame de Namur (SNDs) founded Trinity in 1897 in response to Catholic University's refusal to admit women at that time. The SNDs are a two-hundred-year-old international congregation of religious women with a distinctive mission to the education of women and girls and service to the poor. For most of its first century, Trinity educated a relatively

NEW DIRECTIONS FOR HIGHER EDUCATION • DOI: 10.1002/he

small population of academically talented middle-class Catholic women. As women's colleges declined in the face of coeducation in the latter quarter of the twentieth century, Trinity experienced significant enrollment and financial challenges, leading to a major institutional crisis in the late 1980s.

In 1987, Trinity's president resigned after a long-simmering dispute with the faculty over the need for institutional change. Shortly after the president's departure, a small team from the Middle States Association of Colleges and Schools, Trinity's regional accrediting commission, visited Trinity with a specific request to meet with the board of trustees. The team chair made it clear from her opening statement to the trustees that this was not a social call.

Accompanying the team chair was the Middle States Association staff liaison assigned to Trinity, a thoughtful academic who was exasperated with the events leading up to the visit, the culmination of more than a decade of tension at Trinity over declining enrollment, financial instability, and governance struggles. Two full teams had visited in 1979 and again in 1985; that relatively short period between team visits was evidence of the seriousness of the situation. Both team reports from those years urged Trinity to make changes to improve institutional health, such as diversifying programs to attract new target markets and adopting a more welcoming posture toward new student populations. The 1985 visiting team report sharply criticized what that team perceived as profound internal conflict about institutional mission, a struggle between those who longed for Trinity's past and those who yearned for a new future. The team wrote that a common understanding of and commitment to the college's mission statement was essential to developing a clear direction and purpose for the institution. Trinity's crisis only deepened after the highly critical 1985 team report, with the struggle over change eventually leading to the president's resignation in March 1987 and the appearance of the two Middle States Association visitors in Trinity's boardroom. The visitors were blunt: they read a litany of Middle States Association visits and correspondence over the previous two decades that made the case for urgent action. Most trustees were stunned, unaware of the extent to which the accrediting agency had advised Trinity of its mounting concerns about enrollment, finances, and governance. The visitors were especially critical of the board's apparent choice to remain distant from the internal conflict between the president and faculty. Putting down her paper, the team chair looked intently at Trinity's trustees and delivered this final warning: the board must accept its responsibility to resolve Trinity's long crisis or prepare to close the college.

In some shock, the board at last began to take action, meeting with faculty, students, and other constituencies to engage the college community in mapping institutional restructure. Board leadership itself changed, and the new board chair led the trustees through a process that concluded with a historic vote to open the search for a new president to lay leadership after eighty-seven years of religious sisters in the presidency. A new president, an

NEW DIRECTIONS FOR HIGHER EDUCATION • DOI: 10.1002/he

experienced lay administrator, took office in early 1988, and his inaugura-
tion seemed to launch a new era of optimism and excitement for Trinity's
future.

The optimism was short-lived; the problems with enrollment and
finances continued. In the summer of 1989, another presidential vacancy
led the board to appoint one of its own members, an alumna trustee whose
previous experience was in law school clinical programs and fundraising,
not in senior administration.

Within weeks of this appointment, the Middle States Association staff
liaison was knocking on the new president's door with more bad news: the
accrediting commission rejected a periodic review report that Trinity submitted just before the new president took office; the report had to be redone
in its entirety. More urgent, the accreditors were concerned about the frequent turnover in Trinity's presidency (the latest president was the sixth person in eight years to have presidential authority at Trinity, including interim
leaders); the fact that the board had chosen an inexperienced young lawyer
to take on this difficult case was also a red flag. The visitor then softened
her tone and offered the new president some valuable advice: pay attention
to mission, she said; Trinity's mission is great and necessary. Understand
what the mission truly means, and then let this great mission lead all
actions. She also left a copy of the Characteristics of Excellence, the Middle
States Association standards for accreditation.

Taking the Middle States Association visitor's advice to heart, as well as
the evidence gleaned from the prior decade's worth of accreditation reports, the
new president consulted with the trustees and faculty leadership about moving into a strategic planning process focusing on mission. The president
quickly learned that accreditation standards could be a fulcrum to push the
planning process along. The campus community considered new interpretations of Trinity's historic mission as a Catholic women's college evolving
into a more diversified institution. The planners examined market position
and resource needs, other organizational models, and innovative ideas about
delivering curricula to new types of learners. The campus community eventually reached a broader consensus on the idea that mission should focus
on all women who might benefit from this form of education, not just a particular demographic. Trinity historically served predominantly white
Catholic women of traditional age from the East Coast with moderately high
SAT scores. Today it serves a student body that is 85 percent black and His-
panic women (and men in some programs) of all ages from the Washington
region, and two-thirds are over the age of twenty-five.

With this planning process under way, Trinity submitted the revised
periodic review report in 1991 and received strong affirmation in response
from the Middle States Association. One reviewer of the 1991 report noted
that Trinity's choice to embrace adult education for women broadly was in
many ways more provocative than choosing coeducation. The changing
demographics of Trinity's student body illustrated the truth of this statement;

NEW DIRECTIONS FOR HIGHER EDUCATION • DOI: 10.1002/he

the college community was learning that in order to sustain the historic mission to women as the primary mission, almost everything at Trinity would have to change in curricula and programs to serve a highly diverse, generally low-income, frequently underprepared population of women from the city whose desire for greater empowerment and ambition for change in their own lives led them to Trinity.

In 1992, Trinity adopted a new strategic plan, Toward Trinity 2000, and moved ahead with curriculum reform, master planning, and reorganization into two academic units: the College of Arts and Sciences for the historic women's college and the School of Professional Studies for adult and graduate programs. Enrollment grew, and finances stabilized. Trinity submitted annual follow-up reports to the Middle States Association and received affirmative replies each year.

Then, in 1994–1995, just as Trinity was starting preparation for the 1996 decennial Middle States accreditation review, a serious rift erupted between the college and Trinity's Alumnae Association over the issues of institutional change. Unhappy alumnae complained that Trinity had watered down the liberal arts, accepted too many unqualified minority students, and strayed from true Catholic identity. Some stopped contributing. Many also wrote letters to the president to complain.

Meanwhile, with the 1996 accreditation moment looming, Trinity was preparing a comprehensive self-study using Toward Trinity 2000 as the backbone for institutional assessment. Some of the disaffected constituents felt that this plan created too much change. Before and during the team visit, the unhappy alumnae appealed to the chair of Trinity's Middle States Association team to take action against what they perceived to be the misguided direction of their alma mater. Modeling the best kind of accreditation leadership, the team chair told the agitated president to relax, then listened to the unhappy constituents thoughtfully and proceeded wisely. The subsequent team report strongly affirmed Trinity's direction, commending the strategic plan for reinventing Trinity's mission and programs to accommodate the paradigm shift in the student population.

Among many constructive recommendations, the 1996 team report urged Trinity to get serious about making assessment measurable. Moving into a new planning phase in anticipation of the next accreditation cycle, Trinity created a detailed set of benchmarks using a cohort group of similar institutions. The new strategic plan, Beyond Trinity 2000, included goals with quantitative as well as qualitative outcomes measures. It also reorganized Trinity into three academic units: the College of Arts and Sciences (remaining as the core undergraduate women's college), the School of Professional Studies (moving into full coeducation with undergraduate and graduate programs), and the School of Education (coeducational graduate programs for school personnel). With a more broadly diversified institution came a more ambitious strategic identity: Trinity began to embrace the use of the word *university* to define its new organizational model.

NEW DIRECTIONS FOR HIGHER EDUCATION • DOI: 10.1002/he

Former critics began to take notice, and more positively; Trinity was becoming a larger, healthier institution, and alumnae were supporting in greater numbers and with larger financial gifts. In 2000, Trinity broke ground for the first new building on campus in more than forty years, a new sports center; in 2003, Trinity reached the end of the first complete capital campaign in its history.

In 2006, another Middle States visiting team arrived on campus. Trinity's new self-study again used the institutional strategic plan as the backbone. Twenty years after the 1985 Middle States team criticized the institution for being confused about mission, the 2006 team wrote this:

> The team has experienced in Trinity, at every turn, a mission-driven institution. . . . The team recognizes the impressive congruence of Trinity University in 2006 with the original vision of Trinity's founders in 1897. The team admires and commends the University's rejection of the notion that paradigm shift means abandonment of historic mission. Rather, we discover in the work and vitality of Trinity of 2006, a most obvious continuity with Trinity's 110 year old mission expressed with a renewed relevance and vigor [2006 Middle States Visiting Team Report to Trinity].

Accreditation alone did not make it possible for Trinity to recover from the difficulties of the 1980s to become the thriving institution that it is today. However, at significant benchmark moments during the past two decades, accreditation processes implemented with self-study and the insights of thoughtful visiting teams helped Trinity to forge new pathways to institutional success.

The Trinity story is far from over. The last chapter of the 2006 self-study outlined the latest strategic plan, Achieving Trinity 2010. Without a doubt, a future visiting team will review the results of this plan presented in self-study as Trinity continues to embrace the discipline of accreditation processes to ensure continuing institutional progress.

References

2006 Middle States Visiting Team Report to Trinity College. Retrieved December 6, 2008, from http://www.trinitydc.edu/about/report/Report%20of%20the%20Middle%20 States%20Visiting%20Team%20April%202006%20_2_.pdf
Middle States Commission on Higher Education, *Characteristics of Excellence in Higher Education*, 2006.

PATRICIA A. MCGUIRE has been president of Trinity Washington University since 1989. She has chaired more than a dozen accreditation teams and was a member of the Middle States Commission on Higher Education from 1991 to 1997.

NEW DIRECTIONS FOR HIGHER EDUCATION • DOI: 10.1002/he

3

Accreditation may be the sole opportunity for all parts of an institution to inquire together and in depth about the totality of their mission.

A College President's Defense of Accreditation

Robert A. Oden

Some time back, in meeting with the chair of Carleton College's Parents Advisory Council, a group whose advice and expertise and support has signally advanced the college, I suggested the central agenda item for our upcoming meeting be our preparations for and the schedule of our approaching continuing accreditation process. I could not quite discern if the council chair's response—no words, just a facial expression I had not before seen—signaled horror or boredom. *Next thing the president will suggest,* I imagined him thinking, *is that the Parents Advisory Council count the number of steps in the library or review our plans for repairs to the college's utility infrastructure.*

It was a reaction to similar suggestions I had witnessed at Kenyon College, where I was president for seven years, and at Dartmouth College, where I taught ancient Near Eastern religions for fourteen years. Clearly, adjectives like *alluring, entrancing, scintillating,* and *energizing* rarely come to mind when those within or without higher education are asked to focus on accreditation. I have long imagined that the image formed in the minds of those so asked is rather that of a troop of bureaucrats prepared to march on campus, all wearing sharply pressed black suits, shiny black shoes, and old-fashioned fedoras beneath which peek out eyeshades.

Maybe, I have found myself thinking more than once, *maybe we need a new word for this process.* That is hardly entirely possible, since we need a designation that will describe a process that is quite formal and that will demonstrate to the critics of higher education that we take the process very seriously and work to engage everyone in our broader collegiate

NEW DIRECTIONS FOR HIGHER EDUCATION, no. 145, Spring 2009 © Wiley Periodicals, Inc.
Published online in Wiley InterScience (www.interscience.wiley.com) • DOI: 10.1002/he.333

community in the work we are doing. The right word, the formal designation, remains *accreditation,* so we should continue to use it, but we also should do what this chapter seeks to do: always frame the process well and defend the process with vigor and confidence.

Why Accreditation?

So why should we engage our faculty and students and staff, our trustees and alumni, our parents and friends, in the accreditation process? And why do colleges and universities, especially those of some national standing and with many times as many applicants as places in our first-year classes, need and want to accord high significance to accreditation?

My initial answer to these and similar questions ends with questions. We are a collection of teachers and scholars seeking always to expand the boundaries of what counts as knowledge, promoting our students' learning and learning from them. So why would we not wish to learn all we can about ourselves? What possible objection might we formulate to a process that allows us to discover our strengths and weaknesses, our successes and challenges, our wont constantly to change to meet a changing world? About the only thing we can predict about the future is that the future is unpredictable, so why not work together to shape an education that will prepare our students for such a future?

I can readily imagine several persuasive answers to these questions—answers that are anything but irrational or thoughtless. One might answer that accreditation is hardly necessary since any college or university worthy of the name is planning all the time. Task forces, committees, and strategic planning groups exist beyond ready counting. It is these—those immune to the allure of accreditation might say—that merit our attention and our energy, and we simply do not need the formal, once-a-decade (if things go well) requirements that accompany accreditation, such as that to compose an extensive document, which we then ask a group of visitors to review. Is not this rather like asking the *New York Times Book Review* to review once again the ninth edition of our college encyclopedia when it has already reviewed the first eight editions?

Here is one answer to such responses—something that truly is different about accreditation. It is among the only, indeed perhaps the sole, opportunity we have to inquire together and in depth about the entirety of what we aim to do. Through task forces and committees and the like, we probe discrete aspects of our missions and disparate divisions within our institutions. Thus, it is unusual for colleges and universities to fail periodically to review their curricula, their student retention rates, the first-year experience for their students, their endowment management, and much more. But it is equally unusual to review all of these parts of an institution together, all at once, and in cooperation with one another. That is what accreditation demands, and the opportunity to describe and assess the totality of our mission and how each part of the institution contributes to this mission is a rare opportunity, and one we should seize with alacrity and dedication.

There is a second question of, or challenge to, accreditation. Perhaps the arguments I have set out carry some force, but surely these are most persuasive when we are talking about colleges and universities that are newly founded or are facing obvious financial or enrollment challenges or whose missions no longer correspond to the educational needs of today. And surely these arguments carry significantly less force when the college or university in question is one of obvious national standing.

This is not a straw man or purely rhetorical: one hears with fair frequency that accreditation for the best established and wealthiest institutions, and those most highly sought after by applicants, is hardly as necessary as it is for colleges and universities whose challenges are superabundantly clear, and is perhaps entirely unnecessary. However paradoxical, even perverse, the following statement may initially appear, my own argument is just the reverse. Colleges and universities of national regard, those on the interest list of the most talented students in high school today, are precisely those that can and should most benefit from the accreditation process, from the obligation to ask searching questions of every aspect of their mission.

Nationally prominent institutions are, I have come to conclude, especially vulnerable to some unfortunate temptations. Those temptations I label, inelegantly but not, I think, inaccurately, the temptations of the two "s's" or the two "p's": the temptations of becoming smug and self-satisfied or prideful and parochial. The enemy of first-rate institutions is that of heeding all too readily those bromides or aphorisms that proclaim that enhancing things that are going okay carries risks, so it is best simply to leave these things that are going okay as they are. Plenty of curricula, any number of diversity initiatives, lots of assessments of student learning, and so forth are hardly dysfunctional, but all can use some sustained attention and enhancement.

Opportunities like the self-study exercises behind accreditation can thus be the catalysts to move universities and colleges of singular renown to meddle productively with any number of things that are working just fine but could be better. It is precisely the finest colleges and universities that should always ask of themselves, "Is this the best that we can do?" I cannot hear or utter that query without recalling an oft-repeated story told about Henry Kissinger. One of Kissinger's speechwriters, new to his position, toiled for weeks on the first set of remarks he was asked to compose for Secretary of State Kissinger. One day after he delivered his draft speech for Kissinger, back came the speech with a note attached: "Is this the best that you can do?" Back to work went the speechwriter, and he devoted another full week to a second draft, which once again was returned with the same question. Third effort, same result. Finally, the writer asked to meet with Secretary Kissinger, to whom he said, "Yes, this edition of the speech is the best that

I can do." "Good," came the reply from Kissinger, "If this truly is the best that you can do, then I'll read it." The speechwriter relating this story was very, very good at his job, perhaps the best drafter of speeches with whom Henry Kissinger ever worked. And that is the point of the analogy: the finest of universities and colleges can become too enamored of their many and obvious successes, too convinced of their own obvious excellence, with the result that asking themselves if every part of the institution and every person who makes the university the well-regarded institution it has become is always asking the most probing questions of themselves. Accreditation, rightly framed, wisely posed, forces us to do just this.

Before I move to a quite different perspective on accreditation, I offer one further argument on behalf of a process often seen as unproductively onerous. This argument is based on the observation (a truism to be sure but still accurate) that the pace at colleges and universities is predictably demanding. Institutions of higher learning are hardly alone in this respect, as anyone knows who has observed investment bankers or high school teachers or high-tech engineers at work. Still, there is something about the shape of semesters or quarters, something about the finite periods in which we frame and measure our professional lives, that means that those in higher education work markedly relentlessly, with every task and responsibility subject to time-sensitive demands. This means that getting around to what matters most can be, oddly enough, that to which we never in fact get around to.

A telling example for me is the systematic evaluation by and for a board of trustees or regents. Here too the regular, annual pace of meetings is such that time for sustained reflection on how a board is actually using its time, how a group of trustees is bringing, or failing bring, to bear on a college or university its wisdom and experience, is time that can but rarely be found. Indeed, such time can never be found; it must be made. Another example of a productive task for which time must be made is that of faculty by-laws and other such constitutional matters. These matters do not seem important when all goes well, but they can be of vital and even saving importance when matters go awry, as inevitably they will.

Trustee self-evaluation and careful attention to foundational documents such as faculty by-laws are but two examples of the tasks that urgently need doing but that we persistently postpone. Getting to such urgent tasks can, and usually does, need a catalyst, an agent, a demanding motive. One such motive is that prompted by the accreditation process. In short, when asked to do what we most need to do, we finally manage to create the sustained time to do just what matters most.

Experience as a Evaluating Team Member and Chair

I now alter my direction significantly to ask myself what I have learned in serving with some frequency as a member or the chair of an accreditation visiting team. Indeed, one might preface what follows by asking the following question:

Why would anyone ever agree to such service? It is in no college or university president's contract—and it is truly hard work. I do not know that the leaders of institutions of higher education work any longer hours, face any greater challenges, accumulate any more frequent flyer miles than those leading public companies or law firms, but I do know that the pace is nonstop, the hours beyond prudent reckoning. Why, then, add to these hours by volunteering to devote days to reading self-study documents, studying the publications and records of universities and colleges, and then yet more days visiting these institutions, days in which one meeting follows another, from before breakfast until after dinner?

I have formulated two compelling answers to such questions for myself. First, serving on or chairing a visiting team is a key aspect of an obligation we owe as a part of our commitment to teaching and learning. Accreditation is a process that needs to be done well, and thoroughly and professionally. Even were it not for the voices of those criticizing the missions or costs or results of what happens in higher education, aiding other institutions to assess themselves is discharging an obligation we feel as ourselves the grateful recipients of our own educations. As always, speaking about a task as a mission or a calling risks hyperbole, even invites pillory, but it is speaking the truth. Many of us feel an obligation to education, which remains our most certain hope for the future, and many of us act on this obligation.

The second answer is far more direct and carries many fewer risks in the description. Those of us who volunteer to further the accreditation process do so because of the countless lessons we learn in the process.

So what have I learned in myself and multiple times serving on or chairing visiting evaluation teams? I divide my answer into two parts. First, what have I learned that may be of benefit to colleges and universities coming to the close of their previous accreditation period and facing the prospect of beginning the process anew? The first lesson is that of candor. A university or college does itself and the accreditation process no good and potentially much ill by failing to examine itself honestly, thoroughly, and with searching candor throughout. Our question of our own institution should never be, "What weakness or deficiency or challenge do we wish most to disguise lest it be uncovered by the visiting team?" Rather, it should be: "Which of our many weaknesses or deficiencies or challenges do we want to highlight, most deeply to probe and describe, so that our visiting team members can offer us the most searching and productive advice?"

Why should the imperative to scrutinize our own colleges or universities be necessary? Surely this is what we are going to do anyway and in the absence of any such imperative. In fact, it is not so certain to happen, and for the following reason: most of us who have the privilege of leading institutions of higher learning are well rehearsed in the habit of proclaiming to all who will hear, and especially to our alumnae and alumni bodies, that our institutions are very, very fine and are getting ever finer. It is what we do and what we like to do—this self-promotion in the interest of fundraising and increasing the engagement and the confidence of our constituencies.

In this context, I recall with frequency a comment I overheard from a provost with whom I worked at a college whose president I was. In answer to the question posed to her, "What really is your job?" the provost answered, "My job is to make the college as good as the president says it is." To her answer, I did not object at all. She was dead right: what I did, again and again, and what I do today is to describe in glowing terms the many-fold triumphs by the faculty and staff and students of the colleges I have led. What I do not do, with equal persistence, is to reflect at length on areas of weakness, challenges, and the like.

Put differently, and perhaps less high-mindedly, there is another reason for us to scrutinize ourselves with uncommon candor. It turns out that visiting teams, through their careful reading and many interviews, are going to discover those areas on which we most need to work. Absenting myself, I know how talented, committed, and dedicated are those who serve on visiting teams. These professors, institutional researchers, treasurers, and deans inevitably do come on areas of our mission about which we can speak with the least pride, so we should help them and the process by probing and describing these troubling areas openly and fully and in advance.

Second, those serving on visiting teams swiftly learn just how the accreditation process has been framed by the college or university they are helping to assess. The second lesson learned is thus that it is powerfully important that those leading institutions under scrutiny frame the process not as a necessary and lengthy period of drudgery but rather as a prized opportunity for learning. We are all prone to parochialism and even smugness, and it is only those from without, who do not suffer from the local habits and perspectives and glib analyses, who can most help to free us from the constraints of narrow vision.

Now I turn to what I have learned by participating in the accreditation process that has been of estimable advantage not to the colleges and universities I have visited but rather to myself. My turn here is not, I hope and I believe, as solipsistic as it may seem. Even if I am here using the first-person singular pronoun, my intent is to accent what each of us can learn through such participation.

First, and even if I have long had some general notion of the admirable richness and variety of higher education in the United States, those serving on visiting teams learn just how rich this variety is. Here I am doubtless subject to the same parochial tendencies I have faulted. My undergraduate degree is from a liberal arts college at the heart of a major research university. I served, as assistant professor, associate professor, and professor, for nearly a decade and a half at a liberal arts college. And I have been the president of two liberal arts colleges, so that my own experience is a kind of model of how not to experience anything like the sweeping variety of higher education in America. I have worked to combat this deficiency by serving on visiting teams that devoted long hours to evaluating colleges and universities previously beyond my personal ken: universities that were devoted almost wholly to professional education, small colleges with high ambitions but low endowments, and many, quite different, kinds of institutions, each with inspiring missions but with missions as different from one another as our imaginations might create. It is inspiring, this learning about the variety of higher education in the United States. So learning is a heartening reminder that the glory of American higher education stems largely from our freedom to serve very different students, shape markedly dissimilar curricular experiences for this variety of students, and succeed or fail in seeking to fulfill missions dramatically different one from another.

Other lessons are learned in participating in the accreditation process. The single such additional lesson I note here is a restatement of what I have just written: we learn. We learn how other colleges and universities are succeeding where we have not. We learn new strategies, new tactics, new models, new organizational structures. I have not actually quantified the following with anything like precision, but my own guess is that something like half of the ideas I have attempted to insert into the colleges I have run are ideas I have learned while visiting other colleges as a member of an evaluation team. I have done so without any hint of embarrassment.

None of us is anything like smart or experienced enough to generate all of the new ideas we wish to generate. All of us can and should learn from the differing ways to organize divisions of student life, for example, or the models for how best to incorporate the full faculty in shaping agendas for faculty meetings, or the alternative roles and titles one might assign to administrative colleagues. There are, to be sure, multiple ways to discover the inventive ways in which others have addressed problems we all face, but there are few finer ways than devoting weeks to examining the self-study documents of institutions undergoing accreditation and then devoting days to witnessing these institutions firsthand.

And there are other benefits to participating in a process routinely undervalued and seen too often as an exercise in data gathering and crunching. There is, for example, the singular joy of working with others in and as a team. Here, too, I risk banality, and we can all think of multiple and tired conventions descriptive of teamwork and reminiscent of a high school athletic banquet. But risk aside, what we learn in working for a sustained time on a demanding task with colleagues is nothing if not inspiring. Teams can and do accomplish what no one alone might possibly do. They can and do formulate new solutions to old problems. And perhaps best of all, they can and do have a lot of fun in the process. If we learn of one another's strengths and admirable traits, we learn as well of our multiple areas of narrowness or ignorance. Serving on an evaluating team often is an exercise in humility and often offers sustained opportunities for humor at our own expense.

New Directions for Higher Education • DOI: 10.1002/he

Is the Process Perfect?

If one of the imperatives for any college or university moving through continuing accreditation is that of candor and an openness to criticism and to change, are there aspects of the accreditation process itself that might be criticized and might be changed? Of course, there are, and here are some examples.

First, the process is too lengthy. Focusing on it for something like two or three years can produce productive results, but this is simply too much time away from the time-bound, semester- or quarter-governed teaching and learning that is our mission. My own recommendation is that the entire process be limited to one year: a single year devoted to completing an institution's self-study documents, a visiting team's time on campus, and the accrediting agency's final conclusion and recommendation. Is this possible? I do not know, but I do know it should be tried.

Second, some accrediting agencies recommend or require something I think all should: a preliminary visit by the chair of a visiting team. It is not simply that such a visit allows the chair to organize the team's time on campus most effectively or to arrange for the important details of the visit, such as transportation and the information needed in the team's workroom. It is rather, and more important, that the college or university thus visited by the team chair gains a human face; it is that one begins to come to know those with whom the team will soon be speaking. This is important because we all shape and receive criticism better and more fruitfully from those we have come to know and trust. Personal knowledge enhances objectivity in assessment.

Third, my own view is that we have just begun to take advantage of today's radically enhanced technology in the accreditation process. Much more can be done more thoroughly and more effectively were we to ask ourselves systematically how electronic communication and data gathering and sorting and more might aid this process. My recommendation here is that some kind of task force, to include chiefly those in information technology and institutional research, could face just this question far more effectively than can individual institutions or visiting teams. It is easy to imagine a set of guidelines for the efficient and meaningful use of up-to-date technology that might measurably strengthen the entire accreditation process. It is much less easy to create these guidelines, but it can and should be done.

Finally, I often think that it would be good to demand something like special emphasis reports from every college or university undergoing accreditation. Institutions might choose to give emphasis to their general education curriculum or to graduate education or to student learning in the co-curriculum. Such reports are often allowed or recommended but rarely demanded. Were we all required to produce these special emphasis reports, I think we would pay greater heed to the imperative to be candid and resolutely unsparing in our self-scrutiny.

NEW DIRECTIONS FOR HIGHER EDUCATION • DOI: 10.1002/he

Conclusion

So, is the accreditation process more than the laborious creation of an imposing set of documents followed by a lengthy book review? The answer is wholly dependent on how the process is framed. Framed positively, as a rare opportunity to learn about ourselves, the process is worth it. It produces multiple benefits that continue long after and far beyond the accreditation process itself. The framing is up to those of us who are fortunate enough to lead higher education in the United States—an education that remains, despite many challenges internal and external, despite the striking advances in higher education across the globe, an envied model for those beyond our shores.

ROBERT A. ODEN *is the president of Carleton College in Northfield, Minnesota.*

NEW DIRECTIONS FOR HIGHER EDUCATION • DOI: 10.1002/he

4

In the current environment, presidents and chancellors can expect to have their institutions under nearly continuous scrutiny from regional accrediting bodies.

The Impact of the Changing Climate for Accreditation on the Individual College or University: Five Trends and Their Implications

John W. Bardo

It was only a few years ago that regional accreditation was an episode in a higher education institution's life. Every ten years, the institution would gear up for a self-study; the accrediting team would visit; the institution would provide final responses; accreditation would be voted; and the institution would "return to normal." Those days are past. Now, presidents and chancellors can expect to have their institutions under nearly continuous scrutiny by regional accrediting bodies. The number of reports, the expected details of outcomes measures, and the level of ongoing interaction between the institution and the regional association will continue to increase. In fact, presidents and chancellors need to plan for the organization, costs, and processes that will be a part of each year's operations as the level of accountability increases.

    This chapter focuses on the impact of the critical changes in accreditation processes and expectations on the role of senior administration and faculty members at the campus level. Of particular importance are the concepts of (1) the changing accreditation climate, (2) the need to focus on assessment across all areas of the institution, (3) organizational approaches to continuing accreditation, and (4) developing a culture of accreditation across the campus that traditionally was found only in professional colleges and schools.

New Directions for Higher Education, no. 145, Spring 2009 © Wiley Periodicals, Inc.
Published online in Wiley InterScience (www.interscience.wiley.com) • DOI: 10.1002/he.334

Key National Issues in Accreditation

The Spellings Commission report, *A Test of Leadership: Charting the future of U.S. Higher Education* (Commission on the Future of Higher Education, 2006), has been taken as a major wake-up call for both higher education institutions and the regional accrediting bodies. The report may have been the most visible indicator of the changing landscape of accreditation, but it was far from the first. Two other trends are much more important, and much more fundamental, than that report: a high level of concern with higher education costs, productivity, and outcomes that cuts across the political spectrum and a shift by regional associations, and higher education itself, to accreditation standards that are much more outcomes based than in the past.

The Spellings Commission report has a specific agenda with both practical and political implications. As a political outcome, it placed the U.S. Department of Education and the federal government in a much more aggressive stance with regard to potentially broadly regulating higher education—a role that in most regards had resided with the states. This effort to assert federal control of "accountability" led to a number of visible discussions in Congress, the professional associations, and among accreditors regarding the changed nature of the federal role in higher education. And as Robert Zemsky (2007) has noted, the commission's most important work may simply have been that it caused others to join the conversation and talk seriously about the national condition of higher education: "I also came to understand just how important it was to begin talking, in almost singular terms, about an American higher-education system—huge, complex, diverse, but nonetheless interconnected by the workings of the market, by a plethora of federal programs of student aid, and by the machinations of accreditation" (p. 7)

As the national conversation about the role of higher education has evolved, there appear to be broad themes with regard to the future of regional accreditation:

- What will be the balance between government regulation and peer assessment?
- What is the nature of student learning, and how will it be assessed?
- How does credit transfer from one institution to another?
- How can the accreditation process be made more transparent?
- What is the nature of due process if accreditation is denied?

Balance Between Government Regulation and Peer Review. It is clear that members of Congress from both sides of the political aisle are demanding accountability for many aspects of higher education's operations. While the recent change in control of Congress and the White House may affect specific policies and regulations, there is no indication that either party is content with the current state of higher education. Therefore, it is likely that there will be continued efforts to ratchet up regulation of higher education and demand major increases in accountability for student learning outcomes and cost containment. And because of the legal tie between federal financial aid and regional accreditation, it should be expected that the regional accrediting bodies will continue to be used by the federal government as a major instrument to effect change in colleges and universities. That is, the regional accrediting bodies can expect to remain at the center of the higher education storm. And it should be expected that there will be pressure on these associations to incorporate increased institutional regulation. The long-term question, then, is to what extent regional accreditation will be based on federal regulation and to what extent it will reflect the professional opinions and stances of academic professionals.

Reauthorization of the Higher Education Act in summer 2008 gave some sense of immediate direction with regard to the balance between federal and professional control of accreditation (American Council on Education, 2008; University of North Carolina, 2008). Under this legislation, Congress reaffirmed the roles of individual institutions and the regional accrediting bodies in setting standards. It also prohibited the U.S. Department of Education from establishing criteria that instruct the regional associations regarding successful student learning outcomes. In addition, the committee that advises the Department of Education regarding recognition of accreditors was also restructured. Going forward, the National Committee on Institutional Quality and Integrity (NACIQI) will be composed of eighteen members, twelve of whom will be appointed by Congress (six by each house).

The impact of these changes should be significant in the short run in that Congress has inserted itself much more directly into the process of accreditation. Congress also generally reaffirmed the integrity of the current regional accreditation process. At the same time, the pressure on Congress by constituents with regard to higher education costs and value will not decline. Therefore, it should be expected that the impact of Department of Education policy will be reduced, yet the long-term direction appears to be toward more federally based accountability.

Student Learning and Assessment. Regardless of the balance between federal and self-regulation, there will continue to be a focus on increasing accountability relating to student learning outcomes that transcend individual course grades. Sometimes this conversation focuses on the potential uses of standardized testing reminiscent of No Child Left Behind, and at other times, it is more generically discussed with regard to the need to establish clear and convincing evidence of high-level effective student learning. This discussion began long before the Spellings Commission, but the commission's work fueled the conversation. Today most of the regional associations have adopted some form of learning outcomes as part of their accreditation processes. The Western Association of Schools and Colleges, for example, has adopted a twofold process that focuses on institutional capacity and educational effectiveness. The Higher Learning Commission (HLC) created its Academic Quality Improvement Program and the Southern Association of Colleges and Schools (SACS) has established its quality enhancement plan (QEP) (Smith and Finney, 2008). And while these approaches differ, they all share certain characteristics: they focus on improving or enhancing education, they are institutionally driven, and they must be part of a coherent institutional planning process.

It is clear that the current situation with respect to accreditation and assessment represents only an interim position. The issues regarding federal involvement in accreditation, especially as it affects the definition of educational quality, were recently summarized by Judith Eaton, president of the Council for Higher Education Accreditation (CHEA):

> When it comes to defining quality, a single federal schema has not yet emerged. However, some preferences are clear. The indicators of quality that are mentioned most frequently include graduation rates, job placement, course completion, pass rates on licensure and certification examinations, and successful transfer or entry to graduate school. Quality is defined as tangible benefits gained from a collegiate experience. With regard to judging quality, there appears to be a firmly-entrenched belief that external criteria, external validation, or a single set of external benchmarks must be applied to the indicators to make reliable judgments about quality. "External" means located outside of higher education or accreditation. There are also expectations that a single set of indicators judged by a single set of benchmarks can quickly lead to comparability among institutions of higher education—as urged by the commission [2007a, p. 2].

As the national situation continues to mature, the nature of compulsory assessment will change and the amount of assessment required will increase. There will be continuing pressure to document student learning in all aspects of their education, not just with the context of a defined quality enhancement plan. It also should be expected that the accrediting bodies will increasingly be pressured to require institutions to collect assessment data on a much more regular cycle, perhaps even annually. For example, recently SACS initiated a mandatory fifth-year interim report partly to address concerns of the U.S. Department of Education. In previous years, interim reports were required only of institutions that had not fully met one or more accreditation standards.

Transfer Credit. A third major issue is the transfer of credit among institutions. At the federal level, much of the pressure regarding credit transfer has come from the proprietary and for-profit education sectors. However, even within individual states, there is great concern that community college credits often do not transfer easily. And even among regionally accredited institutions, including those accredited by the same regional association, transferring credit is often difficult. From the perspective of the consumer, this issue causes a lengthening of the time to degree. But also from the perspective of many in government, the inability to transfer credit leads to a fundamental questioning of the nature of regional accreditation itself. It can be expected that there will be continuing pressure on institutions and the regional associations to improve the transferability of college credit among accredited institutions.

Transparency of Accreditation. Fourth, accrediting bodies are being criticized because their discussions and actions are private until a final decision is made regarding the accreditation status of an institution. According to Secretary of Education Spellings, "Accreditation remains veiled and confusing even for many within the higher education community. My department and the Congress have heard from many who have little knowledge of how they're being judged. If institutions are placed on probation, they may not know what's required to return to good standing" (Spellings, 2007).

While one can question whether an institution actually does not know what to do to respond to a negative accreditation review outcome, it is clear that the climate is such that there is strong interest in making the requirements for accreditation much clearer. Interest is also increasing in making information about the meaning of accreditation available to prospective students and their parents. Calls for transparency refer to both clarification of standards and the application process and the translation of the meaning of accreditation information to prospective students.

Due Process in Accreditation. The fifth issue also involves negative accreditation decisions. Once an institution is denied accreditation, what rights of appeal does it have? This issue was brought to a head by the case that Edward Waters College in Jacksonville, Florida, brought against SACS. Edward Waters College was denied accreditation in 2004 due to apparent plagiarism of certain parts of its reaffirmation documentation. It filed a federal lawsuit, and SACS and the college negotiated a settlement of the suit that caused SACS to work with the institution for twelve months. According to news reports, the institution made major changes in the administration, and accreditation was restored in 2005 after its work with SACS,

The facts of the case that involved Edward Waters were sufficiently unique that they did not produce major changes in the internal processes of regional accreditation. Recently accreditation was challenged by Hiwassee College in Madisonville, Tennessee. A primary claim in this case, *Hiwassee College, Inc. v. Southern Association of Colleges and Schools* (2005) was that SACS was acting in lieu of the federal government and therefore had certain due process requirements that it had not met. The appellate court recently ruled that SACS was not a "state actor" and that the federal government had not delegated to SACS the authority to terminate federal funding (and for other reasons as well). In addition to its specific findings, the Eleventh Circuit Court of Appeals decided to publish its opinion so as to treat it as precedent for deciding future actions.

These and similar cases have not fundamentally changed accreditation approaches to due process. However, one of the outcomes of the Spellings Commission and continuing federal concern is that most regional associations have reviewed their internal procedures to ensure fairness. There also is acute attention to ensuring that all accreditation decisions follow association processes as closely as possible.

The Higher Education Act as approved provides additional guidance to regional accrediting bodies with regard to due process. Under this legislation, an accreditor's appellate body must be separate from its initial decision-making body, and its members must be subject to an appropriate conflict-of-interest policy. Also, the institution appealing a negative decision based on financial standards must be allowed to present significant new financial information (American Council on Education, 2008).

Like the other issues discussed, concerns regarding due process will continue for the foreseeable future. There also is some discussion regarding the future role of regional accreditation in performing the gatekeeping function for federal financial aid or whether this function should be separated from accreditation (Eaton, 2007b). Whatever the outcomes of these discussions, it is clear that regional accrediting bodies will be under continuing scrutiny by the executive branch and Congress and that the trend lines are well established. Colleges and universities will have to respond.

Institutional Response to Changing Accreditation

Major changes in regional accreditation will require significant responses by colleges and universities. These issues were highlighted in the introductory portion of this chapter as involving the institution's need to develop organizational responses to continuous accreditation and the need to establish a culture of evidence. Based on these institution-level questions, administrations and institutional boards should discuss six areas:

1. How will the institution create a culture of evidence and assessment across all areas of institutional operations including disciplines without separate professional accreditation, but also business offices, student affairs, and fundraising, for example?
2. What are the means that will be used to assess student learning that might or might not incorporate standardized testing?
3. How does the institution map the five core issues with regard to accreditation onto its campus planning processes?
4. What organizational structures are necessary to respond to the continuous accreditation processes that are resulting from the national dialogue? How will the changes in accreditation policies and processes

be integrated into the institutional strategic planning processes, reward structures, and personnel decisions?

5. What are the costs of developing and maintaining the databases and processes necessary to document student learning outcomes and continuous improvement?

6. How does the campus respond to the changing nature of students and the changing landscape of higher education, which now has many players? That is, how will the institution respond to major shifts in expectations regarding credit transfer?

Creating a Culture of Evidence and Assessment. The Educational Testing Service (ETS) has created a concept called a "culture of evidence" (Dwyer, Millett, and Payne, 2006; Millett and others, 2007). Generally a culture of evidence requires an institution to articulate its claims about what is important regarding students and student learning, develop specific evidence regarding students' learning, and assess students' knowledge and skills. ETS makes the further point that to meet many of the current demands regarding assessment, procedures will need to be developed that create comparable assessments across institutions. This position is consistent with many of the federal and congressional concerns regarding assessment. From an institutional perspective, what is most important about developing a culture of evidence is that the institution needs to recognize that all major elements of a student's education are subject to assessment. This issue goes beyond learning in the major and is not solely subject matter based. Therefore, assessment needs to permeate all aspects of the academic enterprise.

A second aspect to a culture of evidence is that while ETS and others focus on student academic learning, assessment will involve all areas of the university. These assessments may entail student learning such as in cocurricular activities, but it also will encompass such issues as customer satisfaction with administrative services. Increasingly these nonlearning aspects of assessment will also require greater emphasis on efficiency and cost containment. And in the era of Sarbanes-Oxley, it can be expected that assessment will extend to the board of trustees as well. Therefore, increasingly broad-based and pervasive assessment can be anticipated on an ongoing basis in all aspects of institutional functioning.

Assessing Student Learning. At the core of all current and future accreditation requirements is the need to assess the quality of student learning. The documents of the various regional associations make it clear that there is no one approach to assessment that is right for every institution. Moreover, the variations among regional bodies clearly show that the regions themselves do not have a common understanding of what approaches constitute adequate assessment and quality improvement. Currently assessment of quality is primarily an institutionally based issue. For example, SACS provides guidance for institutional quality enhancement plans (QEP), but it does not specify the areas that the plan is to cover. Some institutions, like my own, are using the plan to refocus and restructure its undergraduate curriculum. Others are changing one component of their academic program, such as better integrating technology across the curriculum. If the QEP is well designed and well executed, both approaches currently are acceptable.

Over time, it should be expected that the federal government increasingly will require accrediting bodies to include some standardized measures in the assessment program, increase the range of assessment, and increasingly focus on effective gains in student learning on whatever indicators are used.

The critical questions for institutions, then, become how to structure assessments to meet the demands of the accrediting bodies as they are shaped by both changing peer standards and federal regulation. To what extent will the institution rely on standardized measures, and to what extent will other means of assessment be applied? To what extent will the institution develop its assessment approaches before being required to do so? And can developing an integrated, active approach to assessment forestall federal intervention and imposition of mandated approaches?

These are important issues for individual institutions. The Higher Education Act has given institutions the opportunity to affect outcomes assessment on their own campuses, but the processes will need to be more robust than has been traditionally required by regional accrediting bodies. For certain basic collegiate-level educational skills, standardized tests might be an important component of an overall learning outcomes assessment plan. However, there are many other options for colleges and universities that involve what is known as authentic assessment based on qualitative assessments of student learning according to specifically defined objectives. Institutions must realize that the need for robust assessment procedures is way overdue. As institutions, there still is time to develop strong, verifiable assessment procedures that reflect their institutional philosophy, mission, and expectations.

Integration of Accreditation and Strategic Planning. Traditionally universities and colleges have developed their strategic plans in relation to their positions in higher education. Preparation for an accreditation visit has generally required institutions to document their strategic planning process, but rarely have they included accreditation as a core element of the plan. That will change. Accreditation must be a critical element of institutional planning, and as the emphasis on operational and learning assessments becomes greater, the requirements of accreditation increasingly will need to be at the heart of institutional planning and strategy. Accreditation documentation will no longer be a process that requires institutional attention every five to ten years. Therefore, accreditation standards, especially to the degree to which they incorporate increasing federal regulation, are a critical component of the institution's external environment. So how will the institution increase transparency? How will it document learning and other outcomes? How will it handle transfer credit? And how will it nimbly respond to the changing regulatory environment?

For public institutions, the contextual issues associated with accreditation become even more complex than they are for private ones. Accreditation generally responds to broad peer standards and federal regulations. But public institutions also are primarily regulated by the states, and the states themselves are becoming more aggressive in regulation. Therefore, conflicts and competing interests will emerge about state mandates, professional standards, and federal requirements.

One example of specific state intervention into areas that have normally been the purview of faculty is in setting standards for general education. The State of Florida requires "general education" to be thirty-six semester hours taken in designated areas in math, science, social science, humanities, and communication (Florida Department of Education, 2007). Although these areas are generally included in most institutional notions of general education, the state limits programs to these specific areas and limits the number of credit hours specifically to thirty-six. The State of Texas has a different definition of general education. There, general education is composed of forty-two hours, also in specific fields of study (Texas Higher Education Coordinating Board, 2008). Both requirements are embodied in law, and they are not the result of discussions between regional accrediting bodies and individual campus professional educators. Moreover, nationally there is broad discussion both inside and outside higher education about the need to modify general education requirements and possibly include study outside these traditional fields. In both instances, state laws would have to be modified to fundamentally change general education. Moreover, in Florida and Texas, legislators have intervened in the traditional role of university faculty in controlling the basic nature of the curriculum. This level of control may well be justified from a state policy perspective; nevertheless, it changes the fundamental nature of faculty roles.

Another area in which there is strong potential for conflict is specific disciplinary accreditation. Increasingly, states require standardized state-level exams for entrance into many fields of practice. A student can graduate from an accredited program and still not be licensable without passing the specific exam. And increasingly, other states are recognizing exam-based licenses as the basis for acceptance of an individual in practice working within that state. As cost containment becomes a more major issue on campuses across the country, this trend to uncouple accreditation and licensure may well lead to increased pressure to examine the actual value of the disciplinary accreditation itself. That is, to what extent are standards within the profession defined by accreditation, and to what extent are they defined by state testing standards? This issue is not settled, and it can be expected to become increasingly important over the next several years.

These types of changes in the environment will continue, and there will be increasing conflict among various interest groups. To the extent that institutions can incorporate these critical issues into their ongoing planning processes, they will have increased opportunities to respond to outside pressures and find ways to accommodate these competing demands.

Organizational Structures and Institutional Policies. Because of the profound nature of the questions being asked about higher education, it has to be recognized that the outcomes likely will affect other internal institutional policies and practices over time. There are some critical questions with regard to levels of faculty autonomy related to teaching, evaluation, and assessment. To the extent that there are federal or national standards for assessment, those standards will have to be incorporated into the structure of curricula, degree programs, and possibly even the structure of individual courses—a major change for most faculty members. It also is likely that many outcomes of learning that have been held up by higher education as paramount, but are rarely fully defined or evaluated, will need to be operationalized and linked to the specific structure of the curriculum. For instance, the concept of critical thinking is generally viewed as a core outcome of liberal arts–based education, but rarely is there a clear definition of critical thinking and rarely is it assessed. Similarly, collegiate-level writing and communication skills, and the ability to apply them, are often incorporated in specific courses, but most institutions make little effort to ensure that these skills can be used effectively in a variety of settings.

Finally, it is likely that skills not traditionally part of how we in higher education think about our academic programs may well be part of any federal mandate. One example might be the inclusion of so-called soft skills in the curriculum, such as documenting the ability to work in groups, the ability to work independently, and the ability to manage time and complete tasks. It can be expected that institutional approaches to curriculum development, program deployment, and academic assessment will need to be responsive to these changing federal frameworks. And given the current situation nationally, it can be expected that much of this change in approach will be incorporated into institutional accreditation.

Costs Associated with Assessment. Responding to what can be expected to become continuous accreditation review will require institutions to modify their organizational structures and focus additional human and financial resources on assessment, reporting (to increase transparency), and improving institutional performance on outcomes measures. To date, many institutions have increased funding for offices of institutional research and planning, and some have created separate offices of assessment. However, institutions may well require investment in many other areas if they are to meet greatly expanded expectations. For example, at Western Carolina University, we have found that to improve student learning outcomes, it has been beneficial to increase staffing in our center for teaching and learning to include specialists in portfolio and other forms of assessment as well as curriculum redesign. At the request of the University of North Carolina system, the institution is experimenting with the Collegiate Learning Assessment test and taking part in the Voluntary System of Accountability developed by the American Association of State Colleges and Universities and the National Association of State Universities and Land Grant Colleges. To date, none of these initiatives has resulted in significant additional funding, and there is no reason to believe that the need to add assessment instruments or approaches is reaching a conclusion. The costs to individual institutions will be considerable. Yet there also will be interest by the same groups that are pressuring for additional accountability to minimize costs to the students.

Dealing with Transfers and Nontraditional Enrollments. Another key area in which academic decisions have been largely left to institutions or to the states is credit transfer and nontraditional enrollments. Generally regionally accredited institutions accept credit transfers only from other regionally accredited institutions (without further validation). However, some institutions even within a single regional association do not accept credits from other institutions that are accredited by that association. Nationally this is leading to a fundamental question regarding the meaning of accreditation. If regional accreditation does not set an agreed-on framework for quality, then what does it mean? If it does, then how can credits not transfer? This will remain a major issue that will tend to undermine the long-term legitimacy of regional accreditation and prove to be a basis for increased regulation if it is not solved.

Similarly, there is a core issue regarding acceptance of transfer credit from nationally accredited institutions such as the Accrediting Commission of Career Schools and Colleges of Technology and the Accrediting Council for Independent Colleges and Schools. They are pressing the Department of Education to require regionally accredited institutions to accept their credits—which those institutions so far are resisting. Nevertheless, it must be anticipated that these issues will continue to develop and institutions will need to respond.

Finally, it must be expected that institutions will be increasingly expected to accept co-enrollments of students in multiple institutions at the same time. And some of these institutions may well be of types with which traditional colleges and universities have not had relationships, such as online universities or for-profit institutions. This too has major potential to change the nature of a degree and the level of institutional control. So from the perspective of the individual institution, there are several important questions: What will the standards be for credit transfer and multiple-institution enrollment? How will they affect the meaning of receiving a degree from the institution? And how will transfer credit under these circumstances affect an institution's approach to document quality in its accreditation self-study?

Conclusion

Unless there is a major unexpected change in direction, it must be anticipated that all of these issues, and possibly others, will be incorporated into

NEW DIRECTIONS FOR HIGHER EDUCATION • DOI: 10.1002/he

an institution's regional accreditation process. Because of the link between Title IV financial aid and regional accreditation, the importance of regional accreditation, the national concern over the costs of education, and, most critical, concerns regarding the nature of educational outcomes, it is clear that the leadership of higher education institutions will increasingly require negotiation between traditional peer-based assessment and accreditation and increasing national and federal pressures for standardization.

References

American Council on Education. "ACE Analysis of the Higher Education Reauthorization Act." Aug. 2008. Retrieved Sept. 29, 2008, from http://www.acenet.edu/e-newsletters/p2p/ACE_HEA_analysis_818.pdf.

Dwyer, C. A., Millett, C. M., and Payne, D. G. *A Culture of Evidence: Postsecondary Assessment and Learning Outcomes.* Princeton: N.J.: Educational Testing Service, 2006.

Eaton, J. S. "Assault on Accreditation." *Liberal Education,* Spring 2007a, pp. 2–3.

Eaton, J. S. "Here We Go Again . . . Sin, Salvation, and Accreditation." *Inside Accreditation,* July 20, 2007b. Retrieved December 6, 2008, from http://www.chea.org/ia/IA_072007.html.

Florida Department of Education. *Statewide Postsecondary Articulation Manual.* Tallahassee: Florida Department of Education, Apr. 2007.

Hiwassee College, Inc. v. Southern Association of Colleges and Schools. Appeal from the United States District Court for the Northern District of Georgia. April 14, 2008 Retrieved September 29, 2008, from http://www.ca11.uscourts.gov/opinions/ops/200713033.pdf.

Lederman, Doug, "Edward Waters College Regains Accreditation," Inside Higher Education, June 24, 2005. Retrieved December 6, 2008, from http://www.insidehighered.com/news/2005/06/24/waters.

Millett, C. M., and others. *A Culture of Evidence: An Evidence-Centered Approach to Accountability for Student Learning Outcomes.* Princeton, N.J.: Educational Testing Service, 2007.

Smith, V. B., and Finney, J. E. "Redesigning Regional Accreditation: An Interview with Ralph A. Wolff." *Change,* May-June 2008, pp. 18–24.

Spellings, M. "Secretary Spellings Encourages Greater Transparency and Accountability in Higher Education at the National Accreditation Meeting." Retrieved May 30, 2008, from http//www.ed.gov/news/presreleases/2007/12/12182007.html.

Texas Higher Education Coordinating Board. "Essential Core Curriculum Information." Retrieved Sept. 29, 2008, from http://THECB Academic Affairs and Research Undergraduate Education Field of Study.mht.

University of North Carolina, Office of Federal Relations. *Reauthorization of the Higher Education Act: Summary and Analysis.* Chapel Hill: University of North Carolina, Aug. 19, 2008.

U.S. Department of Education. *A Test of Leadership: Charting the Future of U.S. Higher Education.* Washington, D.C.: U.S. Department of Education, 2006.

Zemsky, R. "The Rise and Fall of the Spellings Commission," Philadelphia: University of Pennsylvania, 2007.

JOHN W. BARDO is the chancellor of Western Carolina University in Cullowhee, North Carolina.

5

An examination of the experiences of the Teacher Education Accreditation Council highlights the conflicting and sometimes incompatible expectations for accreditation.

An Accreditation Dilemma: The Tension Between Program Accountability and Program Improvement in Programmatic Accreditation

Frank B. Murray

Because there is more doubt than ever before about the accomplishments of today's college graduates, the public, employers, often the graduates themselves, and others seek assurance that a program's graduates are competent and qualified (Murray, 2000; Ewell, 2008). There is now the expectation that accreditation will give them that assurance. Moreover, nearly everyone seeks this assurance in an accessible manner, devoid of nuance, by some clear and direct criterion and assessment. That there are no such assessments and criteria that currently meet any reasonable standard of validity is only part of the problem (Nicholas and Berliner, 2007).

Flawed Measures

Because all of the known measures of accomplishment in higher education (grades, license test scores, standardized tests, surveys, rates of accomplishment) are subject to documented flaws and distortions, scholars always advocate multiple independent measures of accomplishment, with the expectation that collectively they will converge on an acceptably accurate result that meets a higher and acceptable standard of reliability and validity (Murray, 2008). It is for this reason that the standards of sound assessment practice established by the American Psychological Association, National

New Directions for Higher Education, no. 145, Spring 2009 © Wiley Periodicals, Inc.
Published online in Wiley InterScience (www.interscience.wiley.com) • DOI: 10.1002/he.335

Council of Measurement in Education, and the American Educational Research Association are firmly clear that no high-stakes decision should be based on a single assessment or test result because no single assessment can stand the burden of the required standards of reliability and validity that would be needed to legitimize such decisions. The limitations of a simple measure like program completion rate or passing rates on license tests to measure quality become apparent when we consider the analogy of mortality rates in hospitals. Would we conclude that hospitals with higher mortality rates are poorer than hospitals with lower ones? Large teaching hospitals often have a higher mortality rate than local community hospitals.

When the convergence of independent multiple measures is sacrificed, as it invariably is, for expediency, efficiency, and the economics of a simple single measure, the corruption and gaming of that single measure predictably follow. In fact, Campbell's law posits that the greater the social consequences associated with a quantitative indicator (such as test scores), the more likely it is that the indicator itself will become corrupted, and the more likely it is that the use of the indicator will corrupt the social processes it was intended to monitor (see Nichols and Berliner, 2007). We find this, for example, in No Child Left Behind (NCLB) measures by the public schools or the Title II pass rates by teacher education schools, which went from 70 to 100 percent in a year's time, when many education schools simply converted the state's exit license test into the program's entrance test.

The competence of a graduate, however, is actually the wrong question to ask of accreditation, which takes as its unit of analysis the program, not the individual graduate. Although the collective accomplishments of the students in the program are relevant to the question of the program's quality, accreditation is not the appropriate tool for establishing the competence of any individual. The license or the mechanics of the hiring decision is the better tool for that question.

But even here the problem is compounded in fields like teacher education, where program accreditation is often allowed to be a sufficient basis for awarding a license to any graduate of an accredited or state-approved program, although since publication of A Nation at Risk (National Commission on Excellence in Education, 1983), most states now also require passing a license test in addition to graduation from an approved program. Quality assurance, however, is once again weakened when two putative independent means of establishing quality, accreditation and the license, are conflated and confounded, sacrificing once again the power of their independent contribution to convergence to a false economy.

Value-Added

In addition to seeking assurance about the competence of the program's graduates, the public, legislators, donors, and the funders of higher education often seek assurance that some value was added over the course of the degree program. Did the program actually make any difference, and did the students learn something of value that they did not know before they enrolled in the program? Was it worth the four- to five-year investment of time and resources, or does the return turn out to be quite small? There is often the further expectation that the program accreditor will tell whether value was added as well.

The quest for value-added or individual improvement invokes all the problems associated with the assessment of the individual student's competence because at its core, value-added is little more than the difference between initial and final competence. More problematic is the desire to attribute the value that was added to some feature of an academic program or some activity undertaken by the teaching faculty because that attribution requires a control group of some students who did not take the program or consort with the teaching faculty. Such groups are almost never available for research into the particular factors responsible for the added value conferred by the program.

These demands for assurance about graduate competence and value-added often clash with one valued benefit of accreditation: the continuous improvement of the program, in which the institution uses accreditation to experiment with alternatives, in an environment of peer review and critique where failed efforts are discarded and promising ones strengthened— presumably to every party's benefit. These demands also clash with one historical benefit of, and the original justification for, accreditation: the certification that the program is in fact a higher education program that has the capacity for quality, whether or not it actually acts on that capacity in ways that yield competent graduates, added value, or improved programs (Ewell, 2008). The clash stems from the fact that the exclusive focus on student achievement and value-added can be blind to how each is accomplished and opens the possibilities that they are accomplished through exploitation or insensitive and unethical administration of the program and institution. It may in fact incentivize these possibilities.

An Accreditation Solution

Are there ways out of the dilemma of these conflicting and somewhat incompatible expectations for accreditors? Can there be a coordination of these separate demands in any single accrediting system?

Founded in 1997, the Teacher Education Accreditation Council (TEAC) has attempted such a system. TEAC's system was recognized by the Council of Higher Education Accreditation in 2001 and subsequently by the U.S. Department of Education in 2003 and 2005. It has over 150 members and has accredited over sixty teacher education programs in over forty states. The system balances three factors in a single system: (1) valid evidence that graduates are qualified, competent, and caring teachers; (2) evidence that the program has a quality control system that works as designed and improves program quality; and (3) evidence that the program has the capacity for quality as measured by the fact that a regionally accredited institution is committed to the program (Murray, 2005).[1] TEAC's assumption is that evidence in these three areas provides a sufficient basis for accreditation and the public assurance of the program's quality. The program, in other words, is shown to have the capacity for quality, the knowledge of how to control quality, and the wit to achieve quality results from its graduates' performance.

These three factors are carefully calibrated so that weaknesses in one can be offset by strengths in others, but overall insufficiencies in any one threaten full accreditation. Failures in the evidence of student accomplishment lead to preaccreditation, failures in the quality control system lead to provisional accreditation, and failures in capacity or commitment also lead to provisional accreditation. The more serious deficiencies are those in the quality control system, because provisional accreditation is awarded only for two years, while preaccreditation is awarded for five years. Failure in any two of the three factors leads to the denial of accreditation.

The system also recognizes that none of the currently available measures or assessments in higher education that meet any reasonable standard of validity are up to the task by themselves of ensuring the graduates' competence. Thus, TEAC programs are free to use the measures on which they truly rely in making their claims, which they do publicly and freely, that their graduates are competent. Because no single measure is adequate, programs must employ multiple measures, and because the validity of all measures is suspect, programs must also provide local evidence of the reliability and validity of the measures they employ.[2] Within these constraints, they are free to use whatever measures they rely on to determine program quality. Programs have used novel measures (such as pupil evaluations of student teachers), and TEAC auditors invariably uncover better evidence of the program's claims than the program brought forward (for example, auditors discovered that arts and science departments regularly used teacher education master's students as teaching assistants in arts and sciences courses because they knew their subjects well and received high course evaluations, a fact not known or cited by the education faculty).

The evidence provided by a program must meet a scholarly standard for evidence. This standard requires that the preponderance of the evidence at least be consistent with the claims. With regard to the key and unavoidable issue of the magnitude of the evidence, TEAC employs a heuristic that absent any other standard accepted by the field, 75 percent of whatever scale is presented is a sufficient standard.

TEAC in fact asks the program faculty to take a position on some twenty categories of evidence available in the field and declare whether they have that evidence, whether they value it, and if they do not have evidence in certain categories, what their reasoning is: they do not value it, it is too costly or time-consuming to procure, it is confidential, or they will acquire it in the future.

NEW DIRECTIONS FOR HIGHER EDUCATION • DOI: 10.1002/he

On the whole, programs that seek TEAC accreditation have solid evidence that the institution is committed to the program. Since the institution is regionally accredited, its capacity in the traditional input areas cited in the federal regulations is established. The only question is whether the program conforms to the institutional norms with regard to these input areas of capacity. The evidence for commitment is that there is parity between the program and the institution overall.

TEAC's Expectations and Experience. TEAC expected initially to find evidence for the widely held belief that teacher education programs are out of parity with their institutions, that they are cash cows—high-volume programs run on the cheap whose considerable profits are used to run more costly programs that the institution really values. TEAC has found just the opposite so far: teacher education programs are more costly than the norm owing to required clinical experiences throughout the programs and the funding of cooperating teachers, special library and media collections of curriculum materials, and instructional technology.

The concerns that have been uncovered are more often with faculty's ability to articulate the quality of the program's control systems and with the nature and analysis of the evidence on which the programs rely to support their otherwise confident claims that their graduates are competent teachers. Of more concern, at least at the outset of TEAC's work, was the lack of confidence many faculties had in bringing forth the evidence on which they truly rely and in acknowledging the weaknesses that their quality control system uncovered. However, the concerns are not of the magnitude of those claimed by the 2005 report on education leadership programs conducted by the Education School Project (Honawar, 2006), which asserted that the quality of the nation's teacher education programs is so low that a new accrediting body was warranted to replace the dominant accreditor, the National Council for the Accreditation of Teacher Education (NCATE), which had enabled low quality to be a norm in teacher education.[3] The report in fact was based on case studies of only twenty-eight programs and surveys and interviews of alumni, school principals, and some deans of teacher education schools. Further, the report avoided the usual scholarly conventions in its text (such as precise descriptions of methodology, results, and data analysis).

The sixty-nine programs that TEAC has audited and accredited are a reasonable cross-section of the nation's programs, and in contrast to the sample used in the Education School Project report, all had convincing evidence from multiple sources for their claims that their graduates were competent teachers. The sources were typically grades given by education and arts and science faculty members; license test results; ratings given by students, alumni, cooperating teachers, employers, and clinical faculty members; and faculty evaluations of student portfolios.

The Balance Between Student and Faculty Learning. To illustrate the fine balance between evidence of student achievement and evidence of program improvement, consider one of the early TEAC audits. In this audit, the auditors were attempting to verify the evidence of the program's claims of student achievement, and the audit trail led to some student folders that revealed remarkably low SAT scores. The program in fact had been silent about its students' SAT scores, presumably because of embarrassment at the low scores. As so often happens in accreditation, and despite TEAC's repeated assurances that only unaddressed weaknesses, not weaknesses themselves, were problematic, the program decided to bury its perceived shortcomings and not speak about them at all. It turned out that while the program was disguising what it took to be evidence that weakened its claims that its graduates were competent, it had denied itself the opportunity to provide stronger evidence that it had a robust system of quality control.

What the program had in fact done over the years, in frank recognition of its students' low SAT scores, was to accept the fact that its students, typically first-generation rural college students with English as their second language, were low scorers on the SAT. The program first designed its own study skills measure in an effort to at least accept into the program students who knew how to study. But the home-grown instrument was a failure, and the program shortly gave it up and replaced it with an intensive effort to show its students how to prepare for and pass standardized tests. It aligned curriculum with the state license test, ran workshops on test-taking skills, and paid for practice tests. In the end, these students had nearly the highest pass rates on the state's license tests. By hiding low SAT scores, the program in fact had denied itself the opportunity to present a convincing case for a robust quality control system. It had based program decisions on evidence of student performance: it had shaped responses to evidence of student success and failure, discarded unproductive approaches, refined responses, and gradually improved the program's structure so that it yielded one of the highest pass rates in the state. Thus, the apparent weakness in the evidence for student competence was actually a strength in the quality control system.

In another case, the auditors found that the program's quality control efforts and practices were not systematic but rather idiosyncratic to each faculty member's preferences and style. This weakness was compensated by the very high levels of performance of the program's students owing to the selective nature of the college and the competence of the individual faculty in their subjects and in their personal and tailored, although uncoordinated, advising of their students.

A Balance of Status and Value-Added Claims. A faculty's case for evidence of student achievement requires evidence only about the status of graduates, not how well they perform in comparison to some other group or in comparison to how much less they knew at some earlier points in the program. It is not a value-added case. The claims associated with this evidence, in other words, need not be about the source of the graduates' competence or how much it changed over the course of the program.

NEW DIRECTIONS FOR HIGHER EDUCATION • DOI: 10.1002/he

Claims about cause and growth of student achievement, however, are encouraged and expected in connection with the quality control system as a way of demonstrating the ongoing inquiry of the program faculty into the quality of their program. TEAC expects that the quality control system has evidence that program faculty are curious about the program's effectiveness and its added value and that faculty conduct research into the factors associated with the effectiveness of its program.

The public and employers are largely concerned with only the status of the program's graduates. They want to know whether the graduates are competent, caring, and qualified more than they want or need to know how that competence was acquired, or whether the graduates are more competent than some other group, or more competent than they were when they began the program. TEAC wants to know this as well, but for a different reason: TEAC uses the information as a key ingredient in its judgment of the quality of the program.

The institution and the program faculty, for their part, may be more interested in knowing which attributes of the program contributed to the graduates' competence. Those who enrolled in the program and those who paid tuition and funded scholarships might also have a keen interest in whether any value was added by the program and whether the students showed growth and development over the course of the program. Indeed, in communicating with the public, the program faculty and institution undoubtedly make ambitious claims about the effectiveness of the program and the value that is added from the college experience. This information is captured in the evidence about the program's quality management and control. TEAC wants to know this as well, but again for a different reason: it uses the information as another key ingredient in its judgment of the quality of the program.

A More Optimistic Picture of U.S. Teacher Education

In closing, it is a fair question whether TEAC's approach itself has shed light on the quality of teacher education and whether the collective evidence from its accreditation work is in line with current investigations of the national quality of teacher education. TEAC now has a wealth of data from the programs it has accredited. Some of the findings from this work are newsworthy and counterintuitive. For example, the grades that teacher education students earn in courses in the arts and science disciplines are invariably equal to or better than the grades the arts and science majors earn in the same courses. This finding holds for all kinds of institutions, from flagship research universities to small liberal arts colleges.

As another example, the teacher education students' performance in the clinical portions of the program, the capstone of the program, is strikingly unrelated to their performance in every other part of the program (including the license test scores). The components of clinical performance (ratings by clinical faculty, cooperating teachers, and student teachers) are highly correlated with each other, but they are not related to license test results and grades in the teaching subject and in pedagogy (which are themselves also highly related to each other). These findings hold throughout the country in large and small programs that TEAC has accredited. They present quite a different picture of the health of teacher education than do the typical reports of low-quality teacher education that are found in the recent Education School Project reports and other alarmist reports on teacher education. The TEAC data show that the nation's prospective teachers are quite able in their teaching fields, or as able as majors in those same fields, and they show that there is another dimension to their competence, one seemingly independent of that captured by the typical academic assessments. This dimension is lawful and internally consistent and consistent with the program's claims that its graduates can teach. This other dimension also indicates, at least preliminarily, that schemes for recruiting new teachers that rely solely on subject matter knowledge expertise are likely to be insufficient.

TEAC, as part of its academic audit, has recently begun to ask students, faculty, and cooperating teachers to respond to a series of survey questions about the adequacy of the program: whether certain aspects of the program were inadequate, barely adequate, adequate, more than adequate, or excellent. To date, these survey results indicate, in contrast to the Education School Project findings, that students, faculty, and cooperating teachers rate nearly all aspects of the programs in the more-than-adequate range. And while the ratings are generally high (a score of more than 4 on a 5-point scale), they are not undifferentiated ceiling effects, as there are significant differences among some components in some programs such as technological adequacy or multicultural understanding. The students, however, see their own understanding of their teaching subjects, their understanding of pedagogy, and their ability to teach in a caring manner as somewhat independent of their overall grades in the program and their ratings of the adequacy of the program faculty and courses. They see the adequacy of the faculty and the adequacy of the course, by contrast, as highly related to each other, so it is not that there are not highly correlated dimensions in the survey results, but that the students' view of their own expertise apparently has its sources elsewhere.

These findings indicate that efforts to recruit teachers solely on the basis of their subject matter expertise, a practice often advocated in times of teaching shortages, are likely to be inadequate. At the same time, these findings are not supportive of traditional teacher education programs, whose many requirements cannot be shown in the TEAC accreditation samples to be related to a candidate's teaching competence.

Of course, these findings require further inquiry, as it may turn out that the lack of correlation between the clinical components and the other program components is more parsimoniously attributed to restricted variance, limitations in the coverage, and overlap in clinical and other assessments, or that the lack of significant linear correlation may be due to a threshold effect in which only a certain modest level of academic accomplishment is required for teaching competence, and accomplishment beyond that threshold value has diminishing influence (i.e., the relationship may be curvilinear).

Not all the news from TEAC's accreditation work is encouraging. TEAC bases its accreditation decision on what it calls an Inquiry Brief: a research monograph in which the program presents the evidence it has in support of the hypothesis that its graduates are competent (they know their subject matter, have understood the pedagogical literature, and can teach in a caring manner). To date, all programs have had some difficulty in writing these monographs, which is somewhat surprising as the faculty otherwise regularly publish their own research findings in the scholarly literature. However, their efforts to turn the tools of their scholarship on their own programs often fall below the standard of acceptable scholarship and reveal serious weaknesses in their grasp of research methodology. This finding may be attributable to the segregation of roles in schools and departments of education between those who take responsibility for the education of the next generation of teachers and those who are taking responsibility for the education of the next generation of faculty members in education.

These findings from the audit of accreditation self-studies (the TEAC Inquiry Briefs) have potentially important implications for the design and rationale of teacher education programs, but require confirmation and deeper analysis. More to the point here is that they also support the view that evidence derived from the coordination of program accountability and program improvement can provide an adequate basis for program accreditation.

Notes

1. TEAC uses as evidence for institutional commitment the parity between the program and the institution with regard to the capacity dimensions identified by the U.S. Department of Education (faculty, facilities, resources, student support services, and so forth). The rationale for the use of regional accreditation is that whereas such accreditation demonstrates that the institution satisfies the federal capacity standards for quality, parity demonstrates that the program has satisfied the same standards.

2. Standardized test makers establish the reliability and the validity of their tests for some standardized representative sample. The local program, particularly one that claims it is distinctive, unique, or of higher quality than most other programs, cannot simply assume that the test makers' findings about the sample hold for the students in the program. They must make their own determination by investigating the reliability and validity of these standardized tests.

3. The report did not discuss the newer Teacher Education Accreditation Council, claiming that it was too new and too small to evaluate its impact on the field. TEAC is less than a decade old and had accredited less than fifty programs at the time of the report, in contrast to the National Council for the Accreditation of Teacher Education's seventy-five-year history and its accreditation of about half the nation's thirteen hundred teacher education programs.

NEW DIRECTIONS FOR HIGHER EDUCATION • DOI: 10.1002/he

References

Ewell, P. *U.S. Accreditation and the Future of Quality Assurance*. Washington, D.C.: Council of Higher Education Accreditation, 2008.

Honawar, V. "Prominent Teacher-Educator Assails Field, Suggests New Accrediting Body in Report." *Education Week*, Sept. 20, 2006, pp. 1–4.

Murray, F. "Teacher Education: Words of Caution About Popular Reforms." In D. DeZure (ed.), *Learning from Change*. Sterling, Va.: Stylus Publishing, 2000.

Murray, F. "On Building a Unified System of Accreditation in Teacher Education." *Journal of Teacher Education*, 2005, 56, 307–317.

Murray, F. "Teacher Licensure: Who Should Be Entitled to Teach or How Many Wrongs Does It Take to Make a Right?" In S. Mathison and W. Ross (eds.), *Battleground Schools*. Westport, Conn.: Greenwood Press, 2008.

National Commission on Excellence in Education. *A Nation at Risk: The Imperative for Educational Reform*. 1983. U.S. Department of Education, Washington, D.C. (ED226006)

Nichols, S. L., and Berliner, D. *Collateral Damage: How High-Stakes Testing Corrupts America's Schools*. Cambridge, Mass.: Harvard University Press, 2007.

FRANK B. MURRAY *is president of the Teacher Education Accreditation Council and H. Rodney Sharp Professor of Education and Psychology at the University of Delaware.*

NEW DIRECTIONS FOR HIGHER EDUCATION • DOI: 10.1002/he

6

An external perspective suggests points of convergence and difference between the U.S. and Japanese approaches to quality assurance in higher education.

Accreditation Systems in Japan and the United States: A Comparative Perspective on Governmental Involvement

Rie Mori

The United States is not the only country that has been shocked by A *Test of Leadership: Charting the Future of U.S. Higher Education,* the report released in September 2006 by the Commission on the Future of Higher Education, also known as the Spellings Commission. What the report emphasizes is accountability: the outcomes of higher education or student learning in which taxpayers' money is being spent. It also recommends that accrediting organizations make their standards of accreditation more outcome oriented.

Japan was one of the countries jolted by this report. Consequently the Japanese higher education community has paid significant attention to U.S. higher education since the report was published, for at least two reasons: (1) the Japanese accreditation system was modeled after the U.S. system in many aspects, but (2) it is designed to work under a greater extent of governmental monitoring. In this sense, the commission report, somewhat unexpectedly, seems to follow the idea adopted in other countries including Japan: stronger governmental control over the quality assurance of higher education by clearly demanding that accreditors change the scope of outcome-oriented standards. For these reasons, the higher education community of Japan has a natural interest in finding out whether the report will affect the operation of accreditation in the United States.

NEW DIRECTIONS FOR HIGHER EDUCATION, no. 145, Spring 2009 © Wiley Periodicals, Inc.
Published online in Wiley InterScience (www.interscience.wiley.com) • DOI: 10.1002/he.336

This chapter compares the higher education accreditation system in Japan with the American system, focusing on the extent of government involvement in the processes in each nation.

American Accreditation: Unique Distance from the Government

The American system of higher education accreditation has traditionally maintained a unique relationship with the government: no direct control. This remained true even after the recommendation on the standards of accreditation of the Spellings Commission report, and many discussions toward the recommendation were made known to the public. Because the American higher education accreditation system is largely accepted and traditional, this characteristic of no government control tends to be overlooked. Sometimes the U.S. system is mistakenly thought to be part of a governmental effort. People who have not been involved in the process, including foreign observers, tend to believe that the operations of regional, national, and professional accreditors are based on some type of formal relationship with the federal government. It is true that accreditation by a federally recognized organization has been a requirement for an institution to ensure, for example, its students' eligibility for federal support. In fact, this regulation under Title IV of the U.S. Higher Education Act is widely known not only inside U.S. society but also in the foreign higher education community. However, this regulation of federal aid eligibility should not be taken to mean government control of the accreditation system. The position of the government is not a controlling force but rather a user of a system of accreditation that has been established voluntarily by educators and academics.

Many countries have introduced their own quality assurance systems, taking the distinguished success of American higher education into account to a greater or lesser extent. These systems emerged relatively late, and in many cases in Europe and Asia, they are organized under government leadership, although the ways and the extent may vary. In this aspect of government control, the U.S. accreditation system is probably unique.

Harcleroad (1980) describes the U.S. accreditation system as one of "the American ways of solving new social problems by voluntarily developing new social institutions" (p. 1). This description summarizes the emergence and progress of accreditation in U.S. higher education effectively and eloquently. Harcleroad also emphasizes that the accreditation system was developed by people from high school and college in an environment where colleges and universities had already been established with no central control in order to cope with the problem of articulation between high schools and colleges and that of college choice.

Since this social institution was believed to be working sufficiently, few people, including those outside the U.S. higher education system, expected a

NEW DIRECTIONS FOR HIGHER EDUCATION • DOI: 10.1002/he

drastic change when a national accreditation foundation was proposed in the United States before the Spellings Commission report was issued. Although the proposal engendered lively discussions among educators, accreditors, and policy-makers, this visionary foundation, a centralized accrediting agency under the Department of Education, has not been realized.

What was really defined in the Spellings Commission report was to make accreditation more outcome oriented by altering existing standards. Although the extent of regulation was reduced when the Higher Education Act was reauthorized in 2008, the recommendation of the Spellings Commission report can still be said to be an attempt by the government to introduce major control into the self-regulating community of higher education. From outsiders' eyes, it is therefore remarkable that many regional accreditors had their recognition renewed late in 2007 without changing their standards in accordance with the recommendation. It is interesting to observe that accrediting bodies and the government are contending with each other for social power.

At the same time, important changes can be seen in terms of professional accreditation standards. Some professional accrediting organizations have changed their standards, or interpretations of the standards, by employing comparable indicators such as the pass rates of licensing examinations. This can be understood to be a reaction to some extent to the Spellings Commission report recommendation. It might be true that for some professional accreditation, it is more feasible to use quantitative standards than institutional accreditation, for which qualitative standards are thought to be more suitable.

Japan's Accreditation System

As the discussion was taking place in the United States before (and after) the Spellings Commission report was published, people involved in Japan's higher education community, especially those interested in the accreditation system, observed the direction of the political and academic discourse with keen interest for three reasons. First, they realized that one of the world's most powerful higher education systems might alter its unique way of quality assurance for the first time in more than a century. Second, their own system is based in part on the U.S. system. And third, the United States seemed to be moving toward the strategy that Japan had just adopted.

Background. The current Japanese version of accreditation was legally institutionalized in 2004, but the history of accreditation in Japan is much older than that. The accreditation system was introduced in Japan just after World War II and is believed to be the oldest in Asia. Since that time, the Japanese accreditation system has been modified, primarily modeling itself on the U.S. system. For example, it employs similar operational tactics, especially in terms of institutional accreditation, such as peer review, self-study

NEW DIRECTIONS FOR HIGHER EDUCATION • DOI: 10.1002/he

report, public disclosure, and qualitative evaluation. Nevertheless, there is a substantial difference from the U.S. system: accreditation is mandated by the Ministry of Education for all higher education institutions. These institutions must be accredited every seven years, with the process performed by an accreditation body recognized by the minister of education.

Japan's first higher education accrediting organization, the Japan University Accreditation Association (JUAA), was founded in 1947 during a time when reforms of the education system were taking place under the strong leadership of the U.S. Civil Information and Education Section, an organ of the General Headquarters of U.S. Occupation Forces. JUAA started with forty-six institutions in the country. It was a bridgehead of the American concept of quality assurance of higher education set up in Japan sixty years ago, and it has since functioned as a driving force of quality enhancement of Japanese higher education. However, it differs from the ideal of U.S. accreditation in that membership in JUAA has become selective, so it is something more than proof of meeting a minimum standard. Currently, there are 321 JUAA-accredited institutions (out of a total of about seven hundred higher education institutions that confer a bachelor's degree or higher). Clearly the Japanese accreditation system has developed in a way different from the original concept, which was proof of fulfillment of a minimum standard. It has instead become an emblem of excellence.

Originally quality assurance in the higher education community was primarily the responsibility of the Ministry of Education, Culture, Sports, Science and Technology. Although the system installed in the late 1940s was modeled after the U.S. volunteer system, the Japanese government played the role of gatekeeper in terms of quality of higher education, and the structure of licensing institutions is similar to that used throughout Europe. For example, the use of the term *Daigaku,* which stands for "university" or "college" with the name of an institution, is allowed only when the institution is licensed by the minister of education. One result is that it is difficult for diploma mills to operate in Japan.

In terms of quality assurance, the main strategies adopted by the Ministry of Education were the evaluation of institutions at the point of licensure and control of the total number of students. For the latter strategy, the Ministry of Education limits the number of students that public and private institutions admit yearly. For public, and especially national, institutions, those numbers have been virtually mandated. For private institutions, those numbers have been prescribed, while the trade-off for this restriction on private institutions has been an institutional subsidy. The idea underlying this strategy is that the fewer students who are admitted, the higher the quality of students will be. Therefore, in terms of governmental oversight, the curricula, teaching, and research conducted inside higher education institutions have been given less attention, since licensure was given just once, when the institution was established, with focused monitoring for an initial period of time. After that monitoring period, a Japanese higher education institution is practically ensured a lifetime status of laissez faire, except for monitoring of the number of students. In other words, there is unlimited trust in licensed higher education institutions to self-regulate in terms of quality in curricula, teaching, and research.

Licensure and short-term initial monitoring by the Ministry of Education were the only system of quality assurance of higher education in Japan that received any serious political consideration for several decades.

Development of the System. Major changes in the concept of accreditation started rather quietly. In 1991, self-study and self-evaluation became mandatory when the Standards for the Establishment of Universities, the basic regulation for licensure of higher education institutions, were amended. Self-study is thought to be one of the prerequisites of the U.S. accreditation process, so this amendment was an attempt to import the American idea of accreditation to all institutions in Japan, not just a chosen few.

This amendment of regulation in 1991 was followed by the establishment of a national governmental accrediting organization. This actually came about by reorganizing a preexisting organization operating under the jurisdiction of the Ministry of Education, the National Institution for Academic Degrees (NIAD). It was originally established to confer academic degrees to learners outside the university on the basis of credit matriculation and recognition of educational institutions outside the jurisdiction of the Ministry of Education.

The reorganization of this institution was a result of discussions carried out mainly by the University Council, an advisory committee to the minister of education. A report issued by this council in 1998 recommended the establishment of a national organization for accreditation and advocated university evaluation by "various entities" with "various perspectives." This need for variety is thought to be one of the justifications for the creation of a second accrediting organization and for government oversight of that organization. Although JUAA had been functioning for a long time, it had a limited impact in terms of the number of institutions involved. The report also pointed out that self-study and self-evaluation did not in themselves guarantee the quality of higher education, although they were mandatory for all higher education institutions. Hence, in 2000 NIAD was reorganized as the National Institution for Academic Degrees and University Evaluation (NIAD-UE), with higher education accreditation as one of its missions. Until this time, all changes in policy for quality assurance had occurred as the result of discourse carried out within the academic community.

The next wave of changes in the accreditation process came as the result of pressure from another direction. In 2001, the Council for Regulatory Reform, an advisory committee to the prime minister, issued its first report in which it recommended the establishment of a system of accreditation and recognition of higher education institutions that would allow a third party to periodically evaluate those institutions. This report apparently anticipated a process of accreditation and recognition performed by one entity, but what the Ministry of Education actually created, after a recommendation by the Central Committee for Education was issued by taking the report of the Council for Regulatory Reform into consideration, was a system of "accreditation by recognized organization." In this context, "accreditation" meant "accreditation of higher education institutions by accrediting bodies" as it was understood by the Council for Regulatory Reform; "recognition" came to mean "recognition of accrediting bodies by the minister of education," whereas the Council for Regulatory Reform had intended "accreditation and recognition of higher education institutions by an accrediting organization" in its recommendation. It is unclear whether this was the result of an actual misunderstanding of the objective of the recommendation or an ingenious political strategy by the Ministry of Education to take the entire accrediting system under its leadership. Whichever it was, the School Education Law was amended, and the Japanese accreditation system was reestablished under the guidance of the government.

Current Accreditation System. Changes in the accreditation system in Japan have been abrupt and rather inconsistent. The various changes were causing the accreditation framework to look quite different from that of the U.S. model that had been introduced to Japan more than sixty years before. The main changes were mandatory self-study, creation of governmental accreditation body, and recognition of accreditation by the minister of education.

As of 2008, there are three institutional accrediting bodies in Japan to accredit institutions that grant bachelor's and higher degrees: JUAA; NIAD-UE; and JIHEE (Japan Institution for Higher Education Evaluation), an accrediting body created in 2004 by an association of private higher education institutions. These three organizations also function as professional accrediting bodies in limited fields such as law education, and there are three other professional accrediting bodies recognized by the minister of education. Even so, the number of academic fields covered by the existing professional (program) accreditation organizations in Japan is rather limited.

The Ministry of Education has been encouraging the creation of professional accrediting organizations. At the same time, it has also set up a new rule to allow professional schools to be accredited by foreign professional organizations, designated by the minister of education of Japan, when appropriate domestic accreditors do not exist.

For institutional accreditation, an institution may choose one of the aforementioned organizations (JUAA, NIAD-UE, and JIHEE) as its accreditor. Institutions must go through the process every seven years, but they do not necessarily have to use the same accreditor every time, since, contrary to the U.S. system, the basic idea in Japanese accreditation of higher education institutions does not include the concept of membership. During the establishment of the current accreditation system, the issue of membership was taken into consideration and eventually discarded, mainly because the new system was designed on the assumption that it would allow a governmental

NEW DIRECTIONS FOR HIGHER EDUCATION • DOI: 10.1002/he

organization, NIAD-UE, to step into the process as accreditor. Since all higher education institutions are subject to centralized control by the government, it was seen as inappropriate for a governmental organization, through its role as accreditor, to establish a membership relationship with some institutions and not with others. Hence, the concept of membership was not included in the Japanese accreditation system.

The scope of the evaluation also varies from accreditor to accreditor. Although NIAD-UE and JIHEE evaluate the quality of a higher education institution as demonstrated at the time of the review, JUAA's evaluation considers both the existing condition of a higher education institution and possible changes over the next seven years.

The cycle of accreditation review in Japan is set at seven years for institutional accreditation and five years for professional accreditation. According to the minutes of the proceedings of the Central Committee for Education (2002), it adopted seven years for the cycle of institutional accreditation as an average for the cycle of five to ten years in the United States. After hasty discussion, the Japanese accreditation system instead established one cycle of review for all institutions. Of the three Japanese institutional accreditors, however, only JUAA maintains a policy of midterm subjective review, and this occurs three years after the initial accreditation is granted.

The minister of education's recognition is given only to accrediting organizations that fulfill the following requirements:

- The organization must demonstrate that its standards and procedure for evaluation are reliable enough to grant or deny accreditation.
- The organization must have mechanisms that ensure a fair and appropriate procedure for accreditation.
- The organization must provide opportunities for an institution being evaluated to appeal anything in the accreditation decision report prior to its publication.
- The organization must have a financial basis sound enough to allow evaluation for accreditation.
- Recognition of the organization must not have been rescinded by the minister of education within the last two years.
- The organization must demonstrate that it is free from any obstacles to fair and appropriate decision on accreditation.

These requirements have some points in common with the criteria for the recognition of accrediting agencies by the U.S. secretary of education, and this is not a coincidence. In developing this regulation, Japanese policymakers referred to the U.S. Code, which regulates the institutional eligibility for Title IV of the U.S. Higher Education Act. Significant similarities can be seen in the sections on provisions for appeals or financial sustainability.

NEW DIRECTIONS FOR HIGHER EDUCATION • DOI: 10.1002/he

The biggest difference between the U.S and Japanese ideas on recognition is their purpose: U.S. recognition aims at enabling an institution being accredited to take part in federal support programs, whereas Japanese recognition is related to the fundamental legitimacy of institutions that will be accredited by those organizations. Symbolically, the Japanese government expects recognized accreditors to be part of an institutional accreditation process and ensure that a higher education institution does not infringe on the ministerial rules for licensing of institutions. Accreditation by a recognized accreditor therefore works in part as a review by the licensing body, the government.

The new system of accreditation was accepted fairly readily by higher education institutions once the regulation was established. The idea of quality assurance itself was already widespread in the higher education community, and with Japan's long history of centralized control, institutions are used to mandatory changes.

To summarize the main points of the changes, the recent history of the development of the Japanese accreditation system is one of constitutional ramification, moving away from the U.S. system. What started as an imitation or extension of the U.S. system has transformed itself from a volunteer enterprise to a government-led institution. In the current system, the government is responsible for both direct licensure of higher education institutions and the recognition of accrediting organizations for continuous quality assurance. This increase in central responsibility indicates that accountability for higher education is now regarded as more important than ever before and that both academia and the government are likely to be responsible for that accountability. As a result of the series of modifications of the Japanese accreditation system, it is probably fair to say that although many traces of U.S. influence remain, the system that has been established is truly a Japanese model. This model seems to fall within the Asian context of policymaking in higher education. For example, Korea in 2007 enacted a new regulation for quality assurance of higher education by amending its Higher Education Act, which requires higher education institutions to perform self-study and self-evaluation, empowers the minister of education to recognize accrediting bodies, and allows recognized organizations to accredit higher education institutions. Here we can see an Asian trend of the political changes in higher education that are similar to those that took place in Japan a few years before.

Conclusion

Higher education, which is both a public good and a private benefit, is an integral part of the social structure. It is thus reasonable for a government to pay great attention to its productivity, especially when considerable amounts of public money are involved and higher education institutions at the same time are believed to have an autonomous right to decide who, what, and how to teach and conduct research. The issue of governmental involvement in the accreditation system is not just a question of the method of quality assurance of teaching and research, but also that of initiative in the academic world. In society today, neither the government nor the higher education community has arbitrary power in higher education.

Japan and the United States have experienced major discussions about their accreditation systems in recent years. Japan has introduced a new system of accreditation with governmental recognition, and the U.S. government has stepped forward to try to require accrediting organizations to change the scope of standards. Those changes can be seen in the context of a series of attempts to establish an equilibrium of power between the higher education community and politics. There is probably no lasting point of balance of those forces in a nation, and it may also vary from society to society. The convictions that Japan and the United States have settled on are probably nothing more than compromises. Continuous comparative observation therefore is essential. The central question might be how much these governments will be involved in their accreditation systems and how this involvement will affect the nature of the accreditation process itself and the quality of higher education.

References

Harcleroad, F. *Accreditation: History, Process, and Problems.* AAHE-ERIC/Higher Education Research Report, no. 6. Washington, D.C.: American Association for Higher Education, 1980.

Japan. Central Committee for Education. Commission on Universities. "Minutes of the Proceedings for the Fourteenth Meeting of Graduate Education Section, Commission on Universities." Nov. 22, 2002.

U.S. Department of Education. *A Test of Leadership: Charting the Future of U.S. Higher Education.* Washington, D.C.: U.S. Department of Education, 2006.

RIE MORI is an associate professor at the Faculty of Assessment for Academic Degrees, National Institution for Academic Degrees and University Evaluation, Japan.

This chapter provides an overview of self-regulation of higher education through accreditation, the primary means by which U.S. colleges and universities assure and improve academic quality.

Accreditation in the United States

Judith S. Eaton

Accreditation is a process of external quality review created and used by higher education to scrutinize colleges, universities, and programs for quality assurance and quality improvement. Accreditation in the United States is more than a hundred years old, emerging from concerns to protect public health and safety and to serve the public interest.

In the United States, accreditation is carried out by private, nonprofit organizations designed for this specific purpose. External quality review of higher education is a nongovernmental enterprise. The U.S. accreditation structure is decentralized and complex, mirroring the decentralization and complexity of American higher education. The higher education enterprise is made up of degree-granting and nondegree-granting institutions. These may be public or private, two- or four-year, nonprofit or for-profit. They spend $375 billion per year (Blumenstyk, 2008), enroll more than 17.7 million credit students, and employ approximately 3.37 million full- and part-time people (Chronicle of Education, 2008).

U.S. accreditors review colleges and universities in all fifty states and ninety-seven other countries (Council for Higher Education Accreditation, forthcoming). They review many thousands of programs in a range of

Earlier versions of this material have been published by the Council for Higher Education Accreditation and in Global University Network for Innovation, *Higher Education in the World 2007, Accreditation for Quality Assurance: What Is at Stake?* (Basingstoke: Palgrave-Macmillan, 2007).

professions and specialties including law, medicine, business, nursing, social work, pharmacy, the arts, and journalism.

Both the federal and state governments consider accreditation to be a reliable authority on academic quality. The federal government relies on accreditation to assure the quality of institutions and programs for which it provides federal funds and aid to students. Most state governments initially license institutions and programs without accreditation. However, they subsequently require accreditation to make state funds available to institutions and students. States often require that individuals who sit for state licensure in various professions have graduated from accredited institutions and programs.

Types of U.S. Accrediting Organizations

There are four types of accrediting organizations:

- Regional accreditors, which accredit public and private, mainly nonprofit and degree-granting, two- and four-year institutions
- National faith-related accreditors, which accredit religiously affiliated and doctrinally based institutions, mainly nonprofit and degree granting
- National career-related accreditors, which accredit mainly for-profit, career-based, single-purpose institutions, both degree and nondegree
- Programmatic accreditors, which accredit specific programs, professions and free-standing schools, such as law, medicine, engineering, and the health professions

How U.S. Accreditation Is Organized

Eighty recognized institutional and programmatic accrediting organizations operate in the United States (Council for Higher Education Accreditation, 2008). Accrediting organizations derive their legitimacy from the colleges, universities, and programs that created accreditation, not from government. In 2006–2007, accrediting organizations employed more than 740 paid full- and part-time staff and worked with more than eighteen thousand volunteers (Council for Higher Education Accreditation, 2008).

The Roles of Accreditation

Accreditation carries out four major roles. The first is quality assurance. Accreditation is the primary means by which colleges, universities, and programs assure quality to students and the public. Accredited status is a signal to students and the public that an institution or program meets at least threshold standards regarding, for example, its faculty, curriculum, student services, and libraries. Accredited status is conveyed only if institutions and programs provide evidence of fiscal stability.

New Directions for Higher Education • DOI: 10.1002/he

A second role of accreditation is to provide access to federal and state funds. Accreditation is required for access to federal funds such as student aid and other federal programs. Federal student aid funds are available to students only if the institution or program they are attending is accredited by a recognized accrediting organization. The federal government awarded more than $86 billion in student grants and loans in 2006–2007 (Chronicle of Education, 2008).

Third, accreditation engenders private sector confidence in higher education. The accreditation status of an institution or program is important to employers when evaluating the credentials of job applicants and when deciding whether to provide tuition support for current employees seeking additional education. Private individuals and foundations look for evidence of accreditation when making decisions about private giving.

Finally, accreditation exercises an important role in easing transfer. Accreditation is important to students for smooth transfer of courses and programs among colleges and universities. Receiving institutions take note of whether the credits a student wishes to transfer have been earned at an accredited institution. Although accreditation is but one among several factors that receiving institutions take into account, it is viewed carefully and is considered an important indicator of quality.

Values and Beliefs Associated with Accreditation

U.S. accreditation is built on a core set of traditional academic values and beliefs. Chief among those is the belief that higher education institutions have primary responsibility for academic quality; colleges and universities are the leaders and the key sources of authority in academic matters. Furthermore, accreditation is grounded in the belief that institutional mission is central to judgments of academic quality and that institutional autonomy is essential to sustaining and enhancing academic quality. Another core academic belief is that academic freedom flourishes in an environment of academic leadership of institutions. Finally, in the United States, there is widespread recognition that the higher education enterprise and society thrive on decentralization and diversity of institutional purpose and mission.

How U.S. Accreditation Is Funded

Accrediting organizations are funded primarily by annual dues from institutions and programs that are accredited and fees that institutions and programs pay for accreditation reviews. In some instances, an accrediting organization may receive financial assistance from sponsoring organizations. Accrediting organizations sometimes obtain funds for special initiatives from government or private foundations. Accrediting organizations report that they spent approximately $92 million in 2006–2007 (Council for Higher Education Accreditation, 2008).

Accreditation Review

Accreditation of institutions and programs takes place on a cycle that may range from every few years to as many as ten years. Accreditation, however, is ongoing; the initial earning of accreditation is not entry to an indefinite accredited status. Periodic review is a fact of life for accredited institutions and programs, and self-accreditation is not an option.

An institution or program seeking accreditation must go through a number of steps stipulated by an accrediting organization. They include preparation of evidence of accomplishment by the institution or program, scrutiny of this evidence and a site visit by faculty and administrative peers, and action to determine accreditation status by the accrediting organization.

In the first step of the process, self-study, institutions and programs prepare a written summary of performance, based on accrediting organizations' standards. The second step is peer review, often accomplished through a site visit. Accreditation review is conducted primarily by faculty and administrative peers in the profession. These colleagues review the self-study and serve on visiting teams that review institutions and programs after the self-study is completed. Peers constitute the majority of members of the accrediting commissions or boards that make judgments about accrediting status.

Accrediting organizations normally send a visiting team to review an institution or program. The self-study provides the foundation for the team visit. Teams, in addition to the peers described above, may also include public members (nonacademics who have an interest in higher education). All team members are volunteers and generally are not compensated.

Following the site visit is the judgment by the accrediting organization. Accrediting organizations have decision-making bodies (commissions) made up of administrators and faculty from institutions and programs as well as public members. These commissions may affirm accreditation for new institutions and programs, reaffirm accreditation for ongoing institutions and programs, and deny accreditation to institutions and programs.

A key element of the accreditation process is that it provides institutions and programs with periodic external review. Institutions and programs continue to be reviewed over time. They normally prepare a self-study and undergo a site visit each time.

These steps ensure that accreditation in the United States is a trust-based, standards-based, evidence-based, judgment-based, peer-based process.

Holding Accreditors Accountable: "Recognition" of Accrediting Organizations

In the United States, accreditors are accountable to the institutions and programs they accredit. They are accountable as well to the public and government, which have invested heavily in higher education and expect quality.

Accreditors undertake an organizational self-assessment on a routine basis and are required to have internal complaint procedures.

Accreditors also undergo a periodic external review of their organizations known as recognition. Recognition is carried out either by another private organization, the Council for Higher Education Accreditation (CHEA), a national coordinating body for institutional and programmatic accreditation, or the U.S. Department of Education (DOE). Although accreditation is strictly a nongovernmental activity, recognition is not.

How Recognition Operates. The process of recognition is similar to accreditation in a number of ways. First, CHEA and DOE each develop standards that must be met by an accrediting organization in order to be recognized. Next, the accrediting organization seeking recognition undertakes self-evaluation based on recognition standards, a process that is similar to the self-study prepared by an institution or program seeking accreditation. In addition, CHEA or DOE may require a staff site visit to the accreditor and staff report on the visit. Based on the results of the self-evaluation and site visit, CHEA and DOE award (or do not award) recognition status. Finally, an accrediting organization undergoes periodic review to maintain recognition, just as institutions and programs undergo periodic review to maintain accreditation.

In 2006–2007, nineteen institutional accrediting organizations were or had been recognized by either CHEA or DOE or both. These organizations accredit more than seven thousand institutions that make up U.S. higher education. Sixty-one programmatic accrediting organizations were or had been recognized and accredited more than nineteen thousand programs (Council for Higher Education Accreditation, 2008).

CHEA and DOE recognize many of the same accrediting organizations but not all. Accreditors seek CHEA or DOE recognition for different reasons. CHEA recognition confers academic legitimacy on accrediting organizations, helping to solidify the place of these organizations and their institutions and programs in the national higher education community. Department of Education recognition is required for accreditors whose institutions or programs seek eligibility for federal student aid funds.

Council for Higher Education Accreditation. The Council for Higher Education Accreditation (2006) has six recognition standards by which it reviews accrediting organizations for recognition:

1. *Advance academic quality.* Accreditors have a clear description of academic quality and clear expectations that the institutions or programs they accredit have processes to determine whether quality standards are being met.
2. *Demonstrate accountability.* Accreditors have standards that call for institutions and programs to provide consistent, reliable information about academic quality and student achievement to foster continuing public confidence and investment.

New Directions for Higher Education • DOI: 10.1002/he

3. *Encourage, where appropriate, self-scrutiny and planning for change and needed improvement.* Accreditors encourage self-scrutiny for change and needed improvement through ongoing self-examination in institutions and programs.
4. *Employ appropriate and fair procedures in decision making.* Accreditors maintain appropriate and fair organizational policies and procedures that include effective checks and balances.
5. *Demonstrate ongoing review of accreditation practice.* Accreditors undertake self-scrutiny of their accrediting activities.
6. *Possess sufficient resources.* Accreditors have and maintain predictable and stable resources.

These standards place primary emphasis on academic quality assurance and improvement for an institution or program.

CHEA accreditors are normally reviewed on a ten-year cycle with two interim reports. The review is carried out by the CHEA Committee on Recognition, a group of institutional representatives, accreditors, and public members who scrutinize accreditors for their eligibility for CHEA recognition and review them based on the accreditor's self-evaluation. The review may also include a site visit. The committee on recognition makes recommendations to the CHEA governing board to affirm or deny recognition to an accreditor.

U.S. Department of Education. U.S. Department of Education recognition standards place primary emphasis on whether an institution or program is of sufficient quality to qualify for federal funds for student financial aid and other federal programs.

1. Success with respect to student achievement in relation to the institution's mission, including as appropriate, consideration of course completion, state licensing examination and job placement rates
2. Curricula
3. Faculty
4. Facilities, equipment and supplies
5. Fiscal and administrative capacity as appropriate to the specified scale of operations
6. Student support services
7. Recruiting and admissions practices, academic calendars, catalogs, publications, grading and advertising
8. Measures of program length and the objectives of the degrees or credentials offered
9. Record of student complaints received by, or available to, the agency
10. Record of compliance with the institution's program responsibilities under Title IV of the Act, based on the most recent student loan default rate data provided by the Secretary, the results of financial or compliance audits, program reviews and any other information that the Secretary may provide to the agency [U.S. Department of Education, 2000]

Department of Education recognition review normally takes place every five years. Department staff conduct the review based on communication with the accreditor, a written report from the accreditor, and from time to time, a visit to the accreditor. They also make recommendations to the National Advisory Committee on Institutional Quality and Integrity (NACIQI), an appointed group of educators and public members, to recognize or not recognize an accrediting organization. The committee recommends action to the U.S. Secretary of Education.

How Recognition Is Funded. CHEA funds its recognition activity through annual fees charged to its institutional members. The federal government funds its recognition activity through a budget allocation from Congress to the Department of Education.

Conclusion

Accreditation in the United States is about quality assurance and quality improvement. It is a process to scrutinize higher education institutions and programs. It is private (nongovernmental) and nonprofit—an outgrowth of the higher education community, not of government. It is funded primarily by accredited institutions. Accreditation has a complex relationship with government, especially in relation to funding higher education. It adds value to society through assuring quality, enabling government to make sound judgments about the use of public funds, aiding the private sector in decisions about financial support, and easing transfer of credit.

Recognition in the United States is about scrutiny of the quality and effectiveness of accrediting organizations. It is carried out by the higher education enterprise through CHEA, a private body, and by government through the U.S. Department of Education. CHEA recognition is funded by institutional dues; DOE recognition is funded by the U.S. Congress. The goals of the two recognition processes are different. Whereas CHEA seeks to ensure that accrediting organizations contribute to maintaining and improving academic quality, DOE seeks to ensure that accrediting organizations contribute to maintaining the soundness of institutions and programs that receive federal funds. Despite their different goals, the two recognition processes are similar: self-evaluation based on standards, site visit and report, and award of recognition status. Recognition adds value to society as a vital part of accreditation accountability, or accrediting the accreditors.

References

Blumenstyk, G. "The 375-Billion Question: Why Does College Cost So Much?" *Chronicle of Higher Education*, Oct. 3, 2008, p. A1.

Chronicle of Higher Education. *Almanac Issue 2008.* Washington, D.C.: Chronicle of Higher Education, Aug. 29, 2008.

NEW DIRECTIONS FOR HIGHER EDUCATION • DOI: 10.1002/he

Council for Higher Education Accreditation. *CHEA Recognition Policy and Procedures.* Washington, D.C.: Council for Higher Education Accreditation, 2006.

Council for Higher Education Accreditation. *2007 CHEA Almanac of External Quality Review.* Washington, D.C: Council for Higher Education Accreditation, 2008.

Council for Higher Education Accreditation. *The Condition of Accreditation: U.S. Accreditation in 2007.* Washington, D.C.: Council for Higher Education Accreditation, forthcoming.

U.S. Department of Education. *Current List of Nationally Recognized Agencies and State Agencies Recognized for the Approval of Public Postsecondary Vocational Education and Nurse Education and the Criteria for Recognition by the U.S. Secretary of Education.* Washington, D.C.: Office of Postsecondary Education, June 2000.

JUDITH S. EATON *is president of the Council for Higher Education Accreditation.*

8

The changing landscape of American higher education presents serious challenges to the future of accreditation.

Musings on the Future of Accreditation

Steven Crow

It is quite perplexing that over the past two decades, regional accreditation has been largely on the defensive even though almost all regional commissions underwent the most significant recasting of their standards and processes since the 1950s. In the early 1990s, Congress listened to a long litany of financial aid fraud and abuse and concluded that accreditation had failed to be a trustworthy leg of the quality assurance triad in the United States. Consequently, reauthorization of the Higher Education Act in 1992 included stringent new requirements for any accrediting agency that expected to continue to serve the gatekeeping role for federal financial aid and grants. As further evidence of its disappointment with accreditation, Congress also called for the establishment of new state agencies charged with duplicating some of the work once expected solely, if not primarily, of accrediting agencies. That experiment with the states failed, and accrediting agencies modified policies and practices to meet new federal requirements, particularly requirements about including in accreditation standards clear expectations for achieved student learning.

By the middle of the first decade of the twenty-first century, federal disappointment with regional accreditation had little to do with fraud and abuse and everything to do with a perceived failure to hold colleges and universities accountable for performance, particularly student learning performance. In its report, *A Test of Leadership,* the Commission on the Future of Higher Education (U.S. Department of Education, 2006) gave a stinging condemnation to the efficacy of accreditation, claiming that it not only seemed incapable of setting and implementing high performance goals for

New Directions for Higher Education, no. 145, Spring 2009 © Wiley Periodicals, Inc.
Published online in Wiley InterScience (www.interscience.wiley.com) • DOI: 10.1002/he.338

institutional productivity but it also impeded innovation and change necessary for colleges and universities to rise to the challenge of meeting critical national goals.

One might think that accrediting commissions had been deaf to the calls for change, were captives of outdated approaches to quality assurance, or, as low-budget membership organizations, were too dependent on the support of the member colleges and universities to challenge them in significant ways. Two decades of leadership by regional accreditation commissions in the movement to assess student learning apparently did not count. Recasting of accreditation processes to provide stronger assistance to institutions committed to continuous improvement also apparently did not count. It was easy to conclude that accreditation in general, and regional accreditation specifically, was no longer useful to public policymakers and of limited usefulness to institutional leaders. In the light of this confusing situation, I concluded that this chapter was either to be the draft of an obituary for accreditation or a set of proposals for how it can regain the confidence of college leaders and public policymakers. I chose to write the latter. Although I appreciate the fact that accrediting agencies are short on effective public relations that could change some thinking of their critics, I start with the assumption that changes in accreditation—some significant in their impact—are warranted.

There is still time for the accreditation community to evaluate its contributions to quality in higher education and reform or revise its activities as deemed necessary. Despite the thinking in the early 1990s that the end of accreditation was close at hand, regional accreditation in the intervening years appears to have been able to position itself as still influential in higher education. To some extent, the vigor of the criticism of it and the recent efforts of the Department of Education to reshape it testify to its importance.

Yet even under attack, regional accreditation remains sufficiently embedded in the culture of U.S. higher education that very few people— public policymakers and institutional leaders alike, who can be its harshest critics—can articulate an alternative to it palatable enough to win thoughtful support. The Council for Higher Education Accreditation (CHEA) began its January 2008 annual meeting with a panel charged with exploring the linkage between accreditation and student access to federal aid. When two panelists who advocated termination of that link began to outline their alternatives, even the critics of accreditation as it is currently structured and implemented found the alternatives hard to conceive or accept. Without a dramatic shift in leadership or vision, regional accreditation in the United States will continue for some time.

Restructuring Regional Accreditation

Leaders of regional accreditation have the opportunity to restructure the enterprise to testify to its relevance to quality in higher education.

The future of regional accreditation is in the hands of those who are most committed to it. The leaders—commissioners, board members, and professional staff—of these agencies are smart and thoughtful people. They have proven to be capable of listening to their critics, engaging in serious self-reflection, and creating ways to make self-regulation in higher education effective as times change. If they want regional accreditation to be considered viable, valued, and credible, they will attend to matters they know to be of significant concern. The list that follows is not meant to be exhaustive, and it does not reflect an explicit priority.

First, institutional accreditation needs to be marked by considerably more coordination and collaboration to allow a consistent national voice on such things as national footprint institutions, quality in distance education, mobility of achieved learning, and, if it falls to them, defining a qualifications framework for the nation. As more and more institutions abridge regional boundaries, the need for transparent national coordination grows. As colleges accredited by national agencies offer degrees once the sole domain of regionally accredited colleges, the imperative for stronger national coordination of academic credentials is obvious. A similar challenge is before the specialized agencies as well, particularly those whose programs are inevitably located in larger schools with cross-disciplinary goals such as allied health programs. The recent emergence of several new professional degrees brought home the need to articulate those degrees across a single institution as well as across multiple institutions (Higher Learning Commission, 2006).

Second, all accrediting agencies will have to raise the veil of confidentiality and secrecy. It is an untested assumption that effective quality assurance requires either. Accreditors can and should create a common public reporting template that gives an adequate and understandable summary of what an agency knows and what others should make of that knowledge. This is no small challenge, to be sure, and several viable alternatives have been proposed ranging from a "validated" summary written by the institution to a type of audit statement complete with notations. In the era of Sarbanes-Oxley, if accreditors fail to participate in a reasonable program of disclosure, they will choose to be irrelevant to public policymakers who expect transparency and to institutions and programs that are trying to be responsive to louder and louder calls for transparency and accountability. It might also be noted that emerging international understandings of higher education quality assurance advocate much greater disclosure than is currently practiced in the United States (International Network of Quality Assurance in Higher Education, 2006).

Third, accreditors need to define their basic purpose in terms other than being antigovernmental or being the buffer against government control and regulation. Whether it was Faustian is debatable; the bargain between institutions of higher education and the federal government was made half a century ago when the federal coffers opened to support students and research in colleges and universities. Institutions of all types are subject to all sorts of federal and state regulations and have been for years. The 2008 reauthorization of the Higher Education Act represents a significant increase in federal reporting requirements (Hebel, 2008), so the "accreditation buffer" is more myth than reality, and it has been for at least two decades. Either institutions and programs accept the services of accrediting agencies as being important to the common good and their goals for accountability and improvement, or accreditation will increasingly become marginal to the overriding financial reality of twenty-first-century higher education in the United States. Colleges and universities are heavily dependent on state and federal public funds and on favorable public policy, which is fundamental to their survival. Accreditation might be very helpful in helping institutions respond to demands for accountability; it will never protect institutions from those demands or make them go away.

Fourth, accreditors should revisit what constitutes credible peer review for the twenty-first century. Critics of accreditation as well as some leaders within the accrediting community talk about the growing need to "professionalize" peer reviewers. If that is meant to suggest stronger training overall and targeted training to respond to innovation and change, so be it. If it represents in this time of significant institutional changes the need to involve knowledgeable experts instead of generalists, then that should be done as well. Higher education is becoming amazingly complex in its structures and in its offerings of education and training. An effective peer review team should look different than it did twenty or thirty years ago. But to turn over the process to a cadre of hired full-time professional reviewers deals a death blow to the vitally important synergy of peer review, one of the best-kept secrets of accreditation: that peer reviewers judge, but they also learn and carry that learning back to their own institutions. Moreover, they share that learning within the team and with the institution under review as they move into their next campus visit.

Fifth, accrediting agencies must study whether peer review is threatened if larger groups of stakeholders, such as students, employers, and public policymakers, have greater participation in accreditation processes. In no small part because peer review in many international higher education quality assurance endeavors has expanded to include these stakeholders, U.S. accreditation agencies need to weigh the pluses and minuses of broadening the membership of peer review processes.

Sixth, accrediting agencies, if committed to supporting institutional and program improvement, need to create more low-stakes, high-return opportunities for interaction with their colleges and universities. The Senior Commission of the Western Association of Colleges and Schools and the Southern Commission of Colleges and Schools sought to integrate such opportunities into their multistage evaluation visits. The Higher Learning Commission's AQIP (Academic Quality Improvement Program) is predicated on the importance of such activities. These efforts recognize that it is problematic to load into a single periodic visit, whether decennial or more often, the types of ongoing support that institutions claim they could use and would value. Few accrediting agencies see their work primarily as a compliance activity, yet accrediting processes too often embed compliance in them, making each of them a variation of a high-stakes activity.

It should be noted at this point that the U.S. Department of Education has a very limited perspective on accreditation. Through its regulations, it essentially defines the endeavor as a compliance enterprise; through its application of the regulations, time and again it tries to turn every relationship between a recognized agency and an institution into a high-stakes compliance exercise. Nothing seems to confuse it more than dealing with an agency or an agency's program that embraces quality improvement thinking and methods.

Seventh, almost all accreditation agencies need to figure out new means of financing their operations. As demands build on them, as they expand staffs and invest in technology to respond to those demands, and as they strive to function efficiently in a digital age, they need to find something other than dues and fees to provide their working capital. Obviously they cannot inadvertently follow the Arthur Andersen model, interweaving consultation and quality assurance too closely, but they must find ways to provide a variety of services related to, but not necessary to, their accreditation activities. Some examples are workshops to support assessment, collaborative programming to define effective partnering, and sharing of strategies for the financially fragile.

Finally, institutional accrediting commissions may need to redefine the scope of the enterprise. Are they really accrediting the total institution, or are they accrediting the educational offerings of the institution? For example, does institutional accreditation today testify to the operations of university-owned business incubators or of those customized, noncredit training programs contracted by a corporation, or to patent and licensing arrangements directly related to corporate-sponsored research activities? As the educational institution becomes more and more complex, perhaps it is time for institutional accreditors to acknowledge that they focus on what they know best: quality of education that leads to degrees and credit-based certificates.

The Need to Address National Issues

To achieve several of these goals, the higher education community and the accreditation agencies that serve it will need to study carefully the impact of decentralization on higher education in general and the quality assurance of it in particular. Honoring and maintaining a rich diversity of higher education institutions and programs in the United States, something policymakers and education leaders alike praise, is not necessarily a product of decentralization, nor is decentralization the necessary key to maintaining such diversity. Yet whenever any significant national initiatives (other than federal funding for new programs) are discussed, the almost automatic response from the higher education community places diversity at its core of the higher education enterprise. How in this extraordinarily decentralized system can anyone find significant points of leverage to address national issues? Perhaps the accreditation community can serve as one point of leverage, but that will happen only if a sufficient enough portion of it can agree on an appropriate response to major public policy matters. The challenge is clear in the following three examples.

Student Mobility. How is the higher education community ever going to resolve the issue of student mobility? Some states handle the matter through legislative dictate. Some want federal intervention. But usually everyone is dealing with arguments over transferring outdated measures of learning. Thanks to the Carnegie foundation and other nongovernmental organizations a century ago, many of our current measures of learning and productivity came into being: the Carnegie unit, credit hours, semester and quarter calendars, and so forth (Shedd, 2003). Many experts have argued convincingly that these are out-of-date measures and tools (Wellman and Ehrlich, 2003), but who is empowered by the broader higher education community to study the matter and propose a different system? It is quite clear that no one is willing to let the Department of Education do this work, and it is doubtful that some sectors of the enterprise would accept a national initiative triggered by states. The recent fight over transfer of credits during the 2007 failed negotiated rule making was only in part about the federal role; essentially it was fueled by arguments of institutional autonomy—autonomy from accreditors as well as any other group. Admirers of the Bologna process, which aims to facilitate greater comparability and compatibility among European systems of higher education, suggest strongly that diversity can be maintained even as very basic questions about academic structures and academic quality are addressed across many boundaries (Adelman, 2008).

National Qualifications Framework. Despite Judith Eaton's recent attack (2008) on a national qualifications framework, the nation does need some national strategy to bring order into the disparate credentials our colleges and universities create and award. Take the emergence of the new professional (or practice or clinical) doctorates. Although the Higher Learning Commission concluded that, collectively, such doctorates constitute a new degree-level classification, there is no significant consensus on this. Nor is there any real consensus on what a program in this new degree level should look like, even with the old credit hour measures, let alone the learning achieved in such programs (Higher Learning Commission, 2006). The nation's colleges and universities often are giving degrees with all sorts of titles that essentially define careers, not disciplinary fields or emerging multidisciplinary fields or even competencies basic to the level of the awarded degree. When community colleges threatened to step into baccalaureate education, almost overnight some universities created a new "applied" baccalaureate degree defined less, it seems, by an understanding of what a baccalaureate degree represents other than by a conglomeration of enough credit hours. Bachelor degrees have morphed into master's degrees and into various types of doctoral degrees with almost no thoughtful analysis of what attributes those degrees really represent. Europeans have wrestled with this problem and have created an understandable schema for allowing national flexibility on qualifications within larger European agreements on expected competencies for certain levels of learning (Clark, 2007).

Meeting National Goals. Thanks to the seminal research of George Zook and Melvin Haggerty (1936), accreditation in the United States has focused on institutional mission. This served higher education in the twentieth century quite admirably, and contributed significantly to the diversity of education institutions. For the most part, and often because of federal and state financial incentives, institutions sought to respond to changing national goals without shifting dramatically their missions. With money behind the GI bill, colleges created learning formats fitted to adults. In the 1960s, the enterprise shaped its priorities to fit national defense goals fueled by the Cold War and *Sputnik*. As that decade ended, the community college movement reshaped the opportunities for higher education throughout almost the entire nation. Now the nation has reached an era of diminished investment in higher education yet with dramatic new needs to educate more people, an increasing number of whom are ill prepared to succeed. Short of massive, targeted funding, how do these national imperatives become addressed through so many diverse institutional missions?

In confronting the need to respond to these matters, where are the points of leverage? Very few in higher education want to empower the federal government. Foundations make a difference by attacking parts of the problem, such as K-16 pathways. Some state leaders, both State Higher Education Executive Officers (SHEEOs) and governors, attempt to move institutions in individual states or in clusters of states. Secretary Margaret Spellings thought she could turn accreditation into the major lever for change. But while almost everyone agrees on the need, there is a dearth of leadership in helping highly decentralized systems find solutions.

A New Role for Regional Institutional Accrediting Commissions

This is the challenging context in which accrediting agencies could make noteworthy efforts that testify to their capacity to be respected as well as key players in creating a new balance between national imperatives and the integrity with which colleges and universities must conduct their business. To do this, accreditors must find a way to be the voice of higher education quality assurance in the public policy environment. Although they were created by colleges and universities, institutional accrediting agencies have to be perceived as having a voice related to but distinct from the voice of the higher education community. CHEA is making it very clear that its perspective on accreditation comes from institutions. If fairly represented by CHEA, colleges and universities are skeptical about enhancing the responsibility of accreditation in shaping public policy. During efforts to write the reauthorization of the Higher Education Act in 2008, it seemed to me that accreditors were painted as being either naive or dangerous. But institutional accreditation, because it can serve as a voice of the vast diversity of colleges and universities, is particularly well situated to be a highly effective part of the regulatory triad, and its marginalization, intended or not, must be halted.

Regional institutional accrediting commissions need to coordinate their voices and activities such that they have strong backing and support in asserting their influence in the making of higher education public policy. I suggest five keys to success here.

Give constant attention to the relevance of accreditation processes and standards. Nothing is more difficult for an accrediting agency than changing its standards and processes in some significant way. From the initiation of a major change to its final implementation typically takes at least four years. Federal requirements make greater efficiencies difficult and flexibility and innovation even more problematic. For example, federal regulators tend to expect accrediting agencies to mirror the lengthy kinds of hearing processes when new standards are under consideration. And they seem locked into the perception that most evaluations of an institution must involve an on-site visit. But accreditors can create simpler and more flexible standards to achieve their goals, and accreditors can work with institutions to create a program of interactions that support the dual missions of assuring quality and advancing it. And they can find ways to amend and refine standards and processes other than once every decade or so. When institutional presidents complain about outdated standards and unnecessarily bureaucratic processes, regional accreditation has lost its best advocates.

Show that accreditors have a reasonable sense of when good enough is good enough. When standards were more heavily weighted toward inputs and processes, accreditors seemed to be firm of foot when it came time to sanction an institution or deny or withdraw its accreditation. Now it is time to gain some level of competence with tools of benchmarking to inform judgments about other kinds of performance. Despite some simplistic efforts to measure the effectiveness of accreditation through the number of institutions or programs that fail to meet standards, the real measure of effectiveness should be in the abilities to identify significant shortcomings in institutional performance, and through accreditation to challenge institutions to address them. One institution can argue that its poor graduation rates result from its open admissions, but when its degree productivity is lower than most of the other institutions of its type, then clearly its sense of "good enough" is just wrong.

NEW DIRECTIONS FOR HIGHER EDUCATION • DOI: 10.1002/he

Validate anew the legitimacy of peer review. The significant differences between peer review in the Higher Learning Commission's alternative accreditation process, Academic Quality Improvement Program (AQIP), and peer review in the commission's traditional accreditation program, show that effective peer review can be conducted in more than one way (Higher Learning Commission, 2007). Peer evaluation in AQIP processes, except that done on a small on-site visit, is essentially accomplished through multiple scoring efforts supported by conference calls with participants using a carefully prescribed set of rubrics. The institution never knows who the evaluators are, just the consensus that emerges from the evaluation. Moreover, participants in this peer review process might be experienced implementers of quality improvement programs in business or in state award agencies. In the traditional program, Program to Evaluate and Advance Quality, the informed judgment of faculty and administrators who are vetted by the institution constitutes the peer process. What is most difficult, no matter the process, is finding ways to validate the effectiveness of peer review in accomplishing the commission's goals. Might this be accomplished by having external participants on teams (for example, students, employers, legislative staffers, or SHEEO officers)? Might the required publication of reports or results of visits allow the broader public to evaluate the quality of the evaluation? Is disclosure of the competencies of the team part of this process of validation? Although I doubt that there is going to be much social science in all of this, it is conceivable that greater transparency about the evaluators and their findings will contribute to greater public confidence in their work.

Test long-held conceptions about accreditation. The Higher Learning Commission learned a great deal from its AQIP effort: institutional acceptance of public disclosure; the effectiveness of training institutional teams rather than individuals from the campus; the power of cross-institutional sharing in the training processes; the value of frequent, low-stakes interactions in making a relationship with the commission; and the ease of expanding agency capacity beyond the staff (for example, using train-the-trainer approaches to support the multiple interactions that are part of AQIP). AQIP also suggests that accreditors could probably rely somewhat less on putting people on planes and moving them around, and although marked by considerable use of technology, AQIP has just scratched the surface of how technology might shift the ways in which accrediting agencies could interact with institutions.

Experiment with partnering and collaborating. The accrediting community needs to find more creative ways to share work and responsibilities among accrediting agencies. I propose exploration of shared initiatives with national accrediting bodies, particularly the evaluation of general education. As the defining features between institutions become more and more blurred and as nationally accredited and regionally accredited institutions become more competitive, the higher education community ought not to allow type of accreditation to become a primary definer in the marketplace.

NEW DIRECTIONS FOR HIGHER EDUCATION • DOI: 10.1002/he

Instead, it should share the goal of ensuring appropriately educated and trained graduates who will benefit society. Better success with transfer of students ought not to be the primary reason for for-profit institutions to seek regional accreditation. And regional accreditors ought not be expected to understand, as do many national agencies, how to unravel the corporate complexities marking them. Accreditors need to experiment with some international bridges too in creating and sharing quality stamps that are meaningful across international borders yet are not the same as granting U.S. accreditation.

Conclusion

In this chapter I have wandered rather freely around the changing landscape of higher education in the United States as I contemplate the future of accreditation in it. Sometimes I have written as though accreditation is a coordinated and cohesive entity, and clearly it is not. Sometimes I have turned my eye solely on regional institutional accreditation. But throughout I have proposed that accreditation is and can continue to be as constructive a force in U.S. higher education as the leaders of accrediting agencies wish to make it. Therefore I conclude with my last proposal: lead. Over the past years, I often heard the counsel, "Don't get ahead of your institutions." I would argue that to be effective in the future, regional accreditation must be ready to pool resources, talents, and its collective learning to ensure that it is always ahead, and being there is actually shaping the environment in which U.S. higher education will both flourish and meet expectations of the society it serves.

References

Adelman, C. *Learning Accountability from Bologna: A Higher Education Policy Primer.* Washington, D.C.: Institute for Higher Education Policy, July 2008.

Clark, N. "Bologna: Curriculum Reform and Other Considerations." *World Education News and Reviews,* Mar. 2007. Retrieved December 7, 2008, from http://www.wes.org/ewenr/PF/07mar/pffeature.htm.

Eaton, J. "The Future of Accreditation?" *Inside Higher Education,* Mar. 24, 2008. Retrieved September 12, 2008, from http://www.insidehighered.com/views/2008/03/24/eaton.

Hebel, S. "President Bush Signs Legislation to Renew the Higher Education Act." *Chronicle of Higher Education online news blog* Aug. 14, 2008. Retrieved December 7, 2008 from http://chronicle.com/news/article/4996/president-bush-signs-legislation-to-renew-the-higher-education-act.

Higher Learning Commission. *A Report to the Board of Trustees from the Task Force on the Professional Doctorate.* June 6, 2006. Retrieved September 10, 2008 from www.ncahlc.org.

Higher Learning Commission. *Institutional Accreditation: An Overview.* Chicago: Higher Learning Commission, 2007.

International Network of Quality Assurance in Higher Education. *Guidelines for Good Practice.* 2006. Retrieved September 10, 2008 from www.inqaahe.org.

Shedd, J. M. "The History of the Student Credit Hour." In J. V. Wellman and T. Ehrlich (eds.), *How the Student Credit Hour Shapes Higher Education: The Tie That Binds.* New Directions for Higher Education, no. 122. San Francisco: Jossey-Bass, 2003.

U.S. Department of Education. *A Test of Leadership: Charting the Future of U.S. Higher Education.* Washington, D.C.: U.S. Department of Education, 2006.

Wellman, J. V., and Ehrlich, T. "Re-Examining the Sacrosanct Credit Hour." *Chronicle of Higher Education,* p. B16, September 26, 2003.

Zook, G. F., and Haggerty, M. E. *Principles of Accrediting Higher Institutions.* Chicago: University of Chicago Press, 1936.

In 2008, STEVEN CROW retired as executive director and president from the Higher Learning Commission of the North Central Association of Colleges and Schools after twenty-six years of service, the last eleven as its executive director/president.

NEW DIRECTIONS FOR HIGHER EDUCATION • DOI: 10.1002/he

INDEX

ORDER FORM SUBSCRIPTION AND SINGLE ISSUES

DISCOUNTED BACK ISSUES:

Use this form to receive 20% off all back issues of *New Directions for Higher Education*.
All single issues priced at **$23.20** (normally $29.00)

TITLE	ISSUE NO.	ISBN
_____	_____	_____
_____	_____	_____
_____	_____	_____

Call 888-378-2537 or see mailing instructions below. When calling, mention the promotional code JB9ND to receive your discount. For a complete list of issues, please visit www.josseybass.com/go/ndhe

SUBSCRIPTIONS: (1 YEAR, 4 ISSUES)

☐ New Order   ☐ Renewal

U.S.	☐ Individual: $89	☐ Institutional: $228
CANADA/MEXICO	☐ Individual: $89	☐ Institutional: $268
ALL OTHERS	☐ Individual: $113	☐ Institutional: $302

Call 888-378-2537 or see mailing and pricing instructions below.
Online subscriptions are available at www.interscience.wiley.com

ORDER TOTALS:

Issue / Subscription Amount: $ _____

Shipping Amount: $ _____
(for single issues only – subscription prices include shipping)

Total Amount: $ _____

SHIPPING CHARGES:

First Item $5.00
Each Add'l Item $3.00

(No sales tax for U.S. subscriptions. Canadian residents, add GST for subscription orders. Individual rate subscriptions must be paid by personal check or credit card. Individual rate subscriptions may not be resold as library copies.)

BILLING & SHIPPING INFORMATION:

☐ **PAYMENT ENCLOSED:** *(U.S. check or money order only. All payments must be in U.S. dollars.)*

☐ **CREDIT CARD:**   ☐ VISA   ☐ MC   ☐ AMEX

Card number _____ Exp. Date _____

Card Holder Name_____ Card Issue # _____

Signature _____ Day Phone _____

☐ **BILL ME:** *(U.S. institutional orders only. Purchase order required.)*

Purchase order # _____
Federal Tax ID 13559302 • GST 89102-8052

Name_____

Address_____

Phone_____ E-mail_____

Copy or detach page and send to: **John Wiley & Sons, PTSC, 5th Floor**
989 Market Street, San Francisco, CA 94103-1741

Order Form can also be faxed to: **888-481-2665**

PROMO JB9ND

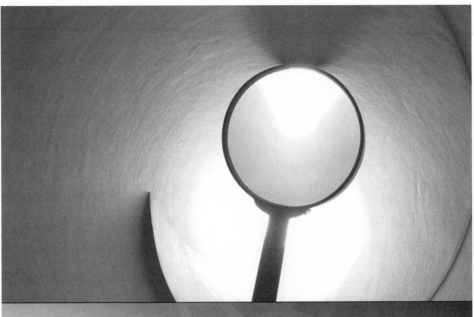

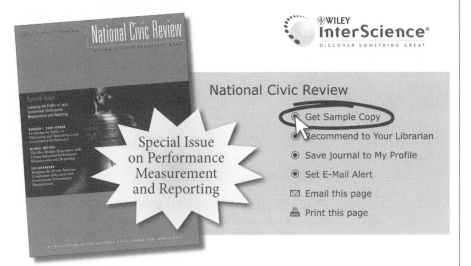